Understanding and Re
the Experience of Dis

CW00344380

Understanding and Responding to the Experience of Disability informs readers about current understandings of disability and ways of recognizing the needs that arise from the lived experience of impairment in schools. While most schools have clear procedures in place with respect to identifying children with special educational needs, the same is not true for disability. Moreover, research suggests that many schools have restricted understanding of this distinction, often equating disability to children with SEN and children with health conditions, thereby failing to recognize the pivotal role of impact.

In this insightful text, Jill Porter argues that disability needs to be understood within the setting in which it is experienced, thereby recognizing that it is not a fixed attributable label, but one that is cultural, contextual and fluid. By providing a theoretical basis for understandings of disability around notions of impairment, experience and impact, the book combines three key components:

- a conceptual understanding of disability – to provide a clear value-driven framework for professional responses;
- an empirical illustration of the development of materials to support an understanding of why the process of disability data collection cannot simply be reduced to two questions on a form;
- embedded illustrative case study material to provide exemplars of how the materials can be contextualized and used to make adjustments to enhance the participation of all children.

Jill Porter is Director of Research in the Department of Education at the University of Bath, UK.

Understanding and Responding to the Experience of Disability

Jill Porter

Routledge
Taylor & Francis Group

LONDON AND NEW YORK

First published 2015
by Routledge
2 Park Square, Milton Park, Abingdon, Oxon OX14 4RN

and by Routledge
711 Third Avenue, New York, NY 10017

Routledge is an imprint of the Taylor & Francis Group, an informa business

British Library Cataloguing in Publication Data
A catalogue record for this book is available from the
British Library

Library of Congress Cataloging in Publication Data
Porter, Jill.
Understanding and responding to the experience of disability /
Jill Porter.
pages cm
1. Students with disabilities--Education. I. Title.
LC4015.P63 2014
371.9--dc23
2014003291

ISBN: 978-0-415-82290-9 (hbk)
ISBN: 978-0-415-82291-6 (pbk)
ISBN: 978-1-315-76331-6 (ebk)

Typeset in Bembo
by Saxon Graphics Ltd, Derby

MIX
Paper from
responsible sources
FSC   FSC® C013056
www.fsc.org

Printed and bound in Great Britain by
TJ International Ltd, Padstow, Cornwall

Contents

Figures

Tables

Chapter 1

Why the need for disability data?

Introduction

A human rights approach has provided the catalyst for schools and other public bodies to review the ways in which their policies, practices and procedures can discriminate against disabled children. A series of legislative acts have provided a common definition, one which identifies the pivotal role of the *impact* of impairment on the daily life of the child. While most schools have clear procedures in place with respect to identifying children with special educational needs (SEN), the same is not true for disability. Moreover research suggests that many schools have restricted understanding of this distinction, often equating disability to children with SEN and children with known health conditions, failing to recognize the pivotal role of impact on daily life. Additionally they may be unaware that some children's conditions are rendered invisible to school through the development of coping mechanisms that limit the opportunity to fully participate in all school activities. *The first aim of this book is therefore to increase policy-makers' understanding of the term disability and to surface the contradictions and tensions that exist.*

A rights approach creates the need for categories – at its simplest disabled or non-disabled – in order to safeguard needs. The World Health Organization's approach to disability suggests the use of finer and finer gradations of categorization can provide a mechanism for collecting and comparing disability data, taking into account impairment, functioning and participation. This however creates an overly bureaucratic system for schools and other services with debatable scientific value. As Rouse *et al.* (2008) state: 'it would seem sensible to develop systems that have the capacity to understand difficulties in the social and educational context in which they occur' (p. 266). In this book I argue that disability needs to be understood within the setting(s) in which it is experienced, thereby recognizing that it is not a fixed attributable label, but one that is cultural, contextual and fluid. Tools are needed therefore which set a child's health condition or impairment within the context of its impact on participation in the home, community and school, AND recognizes the barriers and supports that are in place. *The second aim of the book is to enable policy-makers to go beyond recognizing the need for individual adjustments and respond proactively in making schools better places for learning for all children.*

Understanding disability

Through the Disability Discrimination Act (DDA 1995) we have been provided with a precise definition of disability and this has been reinforced in subsequent acts: namely the presence of an impairment (or health condition) that has lasted for a year or more (or is likely to) and which has a *substantial* effect on daily life. The legal definition was extended in 2005 to include health conditions of HIV, cancer and multiple sclerosis, and these health conditions were recognized from the point of diagnosis. Also covered in the definition are issues of mental health and medical conditions such as HIV and facial disfigurements (highlighting the importance of recognizing that 'impairment' can only be viewed within the context of its impact). While a medical professional might be well placed to identify the presence of a health condition or impairment, disability is experienced and self-disclosed. As a recent document from the Office for Disability Issues outlined:

> Disability is the dynamic interaction between impairment and attitudinal and environmental barriers that hinders a person's full and effective participation in society on an equal basis with others (UN Convention on the Rights of Disabled People) ... Environmental barriers include all the physical and social aspects of the environment that may affect a person's experience.
>
> (Department for Work and Pensions (DWP) 2013, p. 12)

Consequently the same health condition can lead to quite different experiences, albeit that statistically some health conditions are more likely to be associated with disabling experiences. For many children and young people the experience will be highly contextualized, dependent on the social and physical environment. For some both the onset and offset will be gradual, reflecting the fluctuating nature of the impairment or health condition. For others there may be a cyclical element. Given the uncertainties and discontinuities that exist for many people it is perhaps unsurprising that in the adult population only around a quarter of people who come under the Equality Act definition think of themselves as disabled (ONS 2012). As we will see this terminology can have negative connotations as well for children.

Terminology is subject to much debate, the language that is used here is the disabled child, reflecting Gleeson's (1999) view of the importance of putting the oppression first, a political standpoint about the importance of understanding the impact of the environment, including organizational, social and structural aspects, in bringing about change. However one can also infer that the only aspect worth commenting about the young person is their disability, a sentiment that runs contrary to the aims of the book. Chapter 2 will explore the ways in which disability is understood further but here the important message taken from Reindal (2010b) is that 'Disability is something *imposed on top* of the impairment effect, due to ideological, social and environmental consequences' (p. 130).

Disability is a term that is poorly understood in the general population. In the education world there is confusion between the use of the term special educational needs (SEN) and disability. A disabled child only has a SEN if they have a learning difficulty and require special educational provision to be made for them. Previous research by Ann Mooney and colleagues illustrates the ways in which schools and local authorities (LAs) often conflate disability and SEN (Mooney *et al.* 2008). While they form overlapping groups, there are substantial differences. About half of children in mainstream education who meet the Equality Act criteria don't have SEN and equally around half the sample who have special educational needs don't meet the Equality Act criteria (Porter *et al.* 2010). Part of the confusion lies with having different starting places for the conceptualization of these terms. Arguably the presence of an impairment or health condition is the starting point for asking if the child is disabled. For a child with SEN, the starting point is educational need which is linked to the types of specialist support required and the levels of support provided by schools and/or outside services (Wedell 2008). The discourse for one concerns access and participation, and for the other is around intervention.

This distinction however is often overlooked in government publications, where disability is now added to the term special educational needs, to form a new acronym SEND (or, for Ofsted, DSEN). Indeed confusion is evident in the government's own Equality Vision when disability is almost exclusively operationalized in relation to outcome measures for children with SEN. Indeed they describe SEN as a 'proxy' measure for disability (DWP 2012a). In consequence little attention is paid to the disabled child who does not have a special educational need. A particular implication of this is that the government's Equality Vision ignores half of all disabled children. Those who are making average progress are overlooked, their potential for achievement capped. This is an important starting place for recognizing the systemic ways in which partial understanding of disability contributes to the marginalization and disadvantage that is experienced.

Understanding and disadvantage

There can be no doubt that the Paralympic Games in 2012 raised the profile of disability, bringing visual experience of people with a variety of impairments directly into people's homes, in some cases the very first encounter with different bodies. The public has been given the opportunity to witness and celebrate the supreme achievements of sportsmen and women who perform at an elite level. Yet at the same time the media has also revealed scandals of our time, the ways in which disabled people have been harassed and called into account for parking in blue badge bays, how people with learning difficulties have been treated with violence and brutality in homes where the public discourse is one of care. Garthwaite (2011) lists the stark newspaper headlines that 'depict benefit recipients as the enemy in a battle against fairness and responsibility'. A review of changes in newspaper representation of disability by Briant *et al.* (2011) also found an increase in pejorative language and a greater focus on benefit fraud. The report concludes: 'progress on legislation and rights stands in contrast to a relative failure to transform institutions and institutional practices' (p. 14).

While these very public displays of contrasting attitudes are highly evident, there is much less publicity given to the real disadvantage experienced by the disabled child and their family. Recent secondary data analysis by Blackburn *et al.* (2010) has revealed how disabled children are more likely than their peers to live in single-parent families, in poverty, in conditions of material hardship, with poorer health outcomes. Their families are more likely to be in debt and living in rented accommodation. They are more likely than other young people to be bullied (Green *et al.* 2010). They spend more time at home than non-disabled children (Beresford and Rhodes 2008) and their families report difficulty accessing the services they need, to the extent that in 80 per cent of families it causes them anxiety and stress (Brawn and Rogers 2012). Disabled children are more likely to be abused than non-disabled children (Cooke and Standen 2002; Spencer *et al.* 2005). Ofsted (2012) provide data to indicate that disabled children are also less likely to be protected from harm. They reveal how disabled children's needs are under-identified and less likely to be on the protection register – despite often being in contact with a range of professionals. In particular there is often a failure to capture their views and concerns. Disabled young people are less likely to leave school with qualifications and the prospect of employment (Burchardt 2005).

The relationship between disability and disadvantage is also a global concern. The 2010 report on the Millennium Development Goals makes explicit reference (for the first time) to disability, by referring to the marginalization of the disabled child in education. Disability has become part of the mainstream international agenda. The United Nations (2011) raises concern that it is not the person's impairment but their lack of access to resources that is the most pressing issue, their 'disproportionately high rates of poverty' (p. vii). As a result all the Millennium Development Goals are relevant to them. The relationship between disability and poverty is complex (Emerson 2012) but this powerful catalogue of disadvantage clearly demonstrates the need for better safeguards and understanding. Schools have an important role to play both in capturing their views and concerns and helping to safeguard their needs and also in enhancing their life chances through supporting them in reaching their potential.

Disability rights

A landmark treaty, the United Nations Convention on the Rights of Persons with Disabilities (UNCRPD) came into force in 2008 and established disability as a development priority for nations, changing attitudes and approaches to disabled people. It was ratified by the UK government in July 2009, which thereby agreed to its terms including a regular cycle of reporting back to the United Nations, the first of which was issued in 2011. This first report sets out the government strategies for bringing about change, citing the requirement for local authorities and schools to have plans for improving access to the curriculum and to the physical environment with 'a duty to set out how they are improving this access' (Office for Disability Issues 2011). The report also recognizes that this needs to be underpinned by data: 'including ensuring that data collected by different departments can be disaggregated by disability status'. In publishing this report the government held its policies and plans up for international scrutiny and accountability.

The rights of the disabled are given further direction in the recent World Report on Disability where the voice of disabled people frames each chapter (WHO and World Bank 2011). The report culminates in a series of recommendations, translating these to actions for government (as well as for the United Nations). Most pertinent to this book is the recommendation that governments:

> review mainstream and disability-specific policies, systems, and services to identify gaps and barriers and to plan actions to overcome them [and] include disability in national data collection systems and provide disability-disaggregated data wherever possible [and] establish and monitor standards.
>
> (WHO and World Bank 2011, p. 268)

Recognition of the rights of disabled people has provided drivers for changes in policy worldwide.

UK policy

The UK policy landscape has changed quite dramatically over the last 20 years, with a possible high point expressed in the publication of *Aiming High for Disabled Children* in 2007 (DfES 2007) and *We Are On the Way* in 2008 published by the Welsh Assembly (Welsh Assembly Government 2008). These documents set out to transform the provision of services for disabled young people. *Aiming High*, for example, resulted in allocating funding to local authorities in England and Scotland, setting out a clear commitment to:

ensuring that every disabled child can have the best possible start in life, and the support they and their families need to make equality of opportunity a reality, allowing each and every child to fulfil their potential.

(DCSF 2007, p. 3)

Furthermore disabled children were to be made 'a priority at both a local and national level' (p. 6) in the development and provision of services. In 2011 the Welsh government published an update, *The Journey so Far* (Welsh Assembly Government 2011), reaffirming their commitment to uphold children's rights and charting the progress they had made against the agenda set three years previously. In England in 2009 the Lamb Inquiry was set up to report later that year on *Special Educational Needs: Assessment and Funding.* Fifty-one recommendations were made, many of which included reference to 'special educational needs and disability'. The report includes concerns both at the level of information and accountability and the extent to which schools and local authorities were meeting their duties:

It is also clear that there are shortfalls in compliance with requirements for published policies on disability: accessibility plans and strategies and disability equality schemes. Many disability equality schemes are not published. Of those that are published, many do not meet the requirements of the DDA.

(Lamb 2009, p. 41)

Despite the references to the legislation, it is however unclear from the report how the term 'disability' is being used (whether in fact in the place of impairments).

In 2011 the English government published *Support and Aspiration: A New Approach to Special Educational Needs and Disability* and in 2013 draft legislation was released for consultation. The document is entitled *Reform of Provision for Children and Young People with Special Educational Needs* (Great Britain 2012). This document focuses on SEN – except where it makes reference to the Equality Act and to school admissions. Again there is a lack of clarity about the terminology used. A child with SEN is assumed to be automatically covered by the Equality Act and it appears that no other child would be. So, by inference, the child is disabled at admissions whereafter he or she has a special educational need. All children with special educational needs are disabled. The new legislation proposes replacing the current system of statementing and assessments of learning difficulty with a single education and health care plan, co-ordinating support across three services. Quite possibly a child could be in need of a health (or care) plan but not require special educational provision. We turn now to look explicitly at the disability legislation to understand the use of the term and the duties placed on public organizations.

Disability legislation

Over the last 25 years legislation has expanded the requirements from a formal response to disability discrimination to making a more substantive response. There is recognition of victimization and harassment where someone has one of a number of protected characteristics, or is perceived to have. Notably for the topic of this book its origins lie in the world of adults and employment law and much of the advice and guidance for understanding the legislation is provided through government publications and websites.

The definition of disability was set out in the Disability Discrimination Act (DDA) 1995 with a duty placed on schools to take reasonable steps to ensure that disabled students were not placed at a disadvantage. Schools were required to develop plans for improving access in relation to the curriculum as well as the physical environment. This duty was strengthened in the 2005 act by requiring schools to *publish* their plans and strategies in a Disability Equality Scheme and make an annual report. It required schools to be proactive as well as reactive, and take anticipatory steps to ensuring equality of opportunity. It encouraged participation of disabled people in the development of the scheme. It required schools to monitor the impact of their activities and to make reasonable adjustments to policies, practices and procedures.

The Equality Act 2010 replaced the three separate duties on race, disability and gender with a government view that this would reduce the amount of bureaucracy and 'so should be less burdensome and more effective'. It no longer listed the daily activities that the disabled person was required to demonstrate they couldn't do, as had previous legislation, thereby reflecting better understanding of the range of conditions covered by the act. The advice sets out clear guidance in relation to indirect and direct forms of discrimination and harassment:

4.9 Indirect Discrimination: A school must not do something which applies to all pupils but which is more likely to have an adverse effect on disabled pupils only – for example that all pupils must demonstrate physical fitness levels before being admitted to the school.

But with the limiting clause:

unless they can show that it is done for a legitimate reason, and is a proportionate way of achieving that legitimate aim.

4.10 Discrimination arising from disability: A school must not discriminate against a disabled pupil because of something that is a consequence of their disability – for example by not allowing a disabled pupil on crutches outside at break time because it would take too long for her to get out and back. Like indirect discrimination, discrimination arising from disability can potentially be justified.

4.11 Harassment: A school must not harass a pupil because of his disability – for example, a teacher shouting at the pupil because the disability means that he is constantly struggling with class-work or unable to concentrate.

(DfE 2013, p. 18)

The Equality Act 2010 extended the range of adjustments that schools might reasonably be expected to make to include (from September 2012) auxiliary aids and services. The issue of reasonable adjustments is one that taxes both schools and local authorities. Government advice includes the following:

factors a school may consider when assessing the reasonableness of an adjustment may include the financial or other resources required for the adjustment, its effectiveness, its effect on other pupils, health and safety requirements, and whether aids have been made available through the Special Educational Needs route.

(DfE 2013, p. 20)

The advice goes on however:

There should be no assumption ... that if an auxiliary aid is not provided under the SEN regime then it must be provided as a reasonable adjustment. Similarly, whilst schools and LAs are under the same reasonable adjustment duty, there should be no assumption that where it is unreasonable for a school to provide an auxiliary aid or service, for example on cost grounds, it would then be reasonable for the local authority to provide it. All decisions would depend on the facts of each individual case. The nature of the aid or service, and perhaps also the existence of local arrangements between schools and local authorities, will help to determine what would be reasonable for the school or the LA to provide.

And therefore:

what may be reasonable for one school to provide may not be reasonable for another given the circumstances of each case.

(DfE 2013, p. 20)

The focus of this advice suggests that many of the adjustments that are required demand expenditure on additional equipment or services. As our own data revealed however this is a very narrow view of what pupils find supportive. Rather parents report on the importance of the underlying attitude and willingness to make organizational changes that make a difference. Indeed the Life Opportunities Survey also found that the key barrier reported by parents for children with impairment was the attitude of others (ONS 2011b).

One of the strengths of the legislation is that it requires schools to do more than make individual responses. The Equality Act 2010 replicated the requirement for schools and LAs to carry out accessibility planning for disabled pupils. The advice highlights increasing participation in the curriculum, improving the physical environment and making information accessible. Perhaps surprisingly there is no attention drawn to the possibility of any pedagogic or pastoral responses. These accessibility plans may be reviewed as part of an Ofsted inspection. There is however a certain amount of ambiguity surrounding this expectation. At the same time the advice notes:

> It is good practice for schools to keep a note of any equality consideration, although this does not necessarily need to take the form of a formal equality analysis. Publishing it will help to demonstrate that the due regard duty is being fulfilled … They will then need to update the published information at least annually and to publish objectives at least once every four years.
>
> Schools will not be required to collect any statistical data which they do not already collect routinely.
>
> (DfE 2013, p. 24)

The act reduced some of the bureaucratic demands on schools. Schools no longer need to produce an Equality Scheme, instead they need to set 'specific and measureable equality objectives' (DfE 2013). It is therefore hard to understand how schools (or indeed Ofsted) can monitor the effectiveness of their plan, if indeed they do not know who their disabled pupils are. The same is true of course for LAs and their accessibility strategies.

On the one hand schools have been required to be proactive in promoting disability equality by anticipating barriers that pupils could encounter and removing or minimizing them 'to put [disabled children] … on a more level footing with pupils without disabilities' (DfE 2010). On the other hand putting information on a website – the suggested media for publishing plans – has the hallmark of rhetoric if schools are not supported in collecting the very data that would enable them to evaluate their effectiveness. If schools are encouraged to do so then of course this information is also available to local authorities.

In contrast to the conclusion reached during the Lamb Inquiry, research by the Equality and Human Rights Commission indicated that schools have responded to many of these expectations. Almost four in five schools have an Action Plan with targets set, and report actions that have had a positive impact on provision for disabled pupils (Bukowski et al. 2011). The most frequently cited response has been to improve access to facilities and resources; however, it is unclear how schools have gone about identifying disabled pupils and therefore how they can have reached a conclusion about the positive impact. This raises concern about the extent to which advice and guidance has encouraged a compliance or performative response from schools.

The law as a driver of change

The rights agenda so clearly visible in the work of the United Nations is reflected in the Western response to uphold these rights through a legal process. In the UK this has been charted through the evolution of the series of Disability Discrimination Acts. Now encapsulated in the Equality Act (2010) where disability stands apart from other 'protected characteristics' as unlike gender, race, sexuality or religion the emphasis is not simply on ensuring equal treatment but goes beyond this in requiring a change in practices so that the disabled person is able to benefit equally. The discourse is one of equity not simply equality.

Alongside these potential strengths come areas of weakness. As Byrne (2013) has argued in a slightly different context, the law embodies a deficit-based approach to disability. If upheld the law requires adjustments for the individual. The law is also not necessarily the most accessible method for bringing about social change. It presumes considerable knowledge and understanding. Parsons *et al.* (2009a) in a survey across the UK report that only half of the returns from parents indicated that they had heard of the Disability Discrimination Act and around a third knew that it applied to schools. Parents from professional and managerial occupations had more knowledge than other parents. The survey returns suggest that there is also confusion over whether their child is disabled. As the authors state this raises questions about the 'reach' of the legislation and its patchy impact on the rights of parents. Those who do use the law face additional burdens. There can be no doubt that it is a cumbersome and lengthy process, requiring individual applications to develop case law. Runswick-Cole (2007) describes the financial, emotional and health related costs for parents of preparing and attending the tribunal and the ways in which this impacts on family relationships. This complex and time-consuming process is stressful and demanding and even at the end there can still be a gap between the tribunal order and the response of the local authority and school. Even in the case of a desired outcome parents may be required to continue to be proactive in safeguarding their child's needs.

The following description taken from the DfE advice describes the tribunal procedures:

> Claims of discrimination or harassment against a pupil by a school will be made to the tribunal by the parent of the pupil.
>
> 7.7 As with the county court for other types of discrimination, claims have to be brought within 6 months of the act to which the claim relates and the tribunal has the power to consider claims after that time has passed if it considers it just and equitable to do so.
>
> 7.8 If the tribunal rules that there has been a contravention then it has the power to make an order of a remedy which it sees as appropriate. Such a remedy will be with a view to removing or reducing the adverse affect

on the pupil concerned. However, the remedy in a disability case will not include payment of compensation. It is expected that an education remedy will be the most appropriate – for example, if the tribunal finds that a school has discriminated against a disabled pupil by failing to provide extra help needed to compensate for her disability it may order the school to put in place the necessary measures to meet her needs and help her to catch up with other pupils.

(DfE 2013, p. 30)

Parents are unlikely to want recourse to a legal system to pursue the rights of their child unless there is no other avenue open to them and will (in all probability) have already made a formal complaint to the school. At this point it is likely that the relationship with the school has broken down to the extent that the simple introduction of an adaptation or new procedure is unlikely to reconcile their differences and provide a harmonious setting for the education of the child. In fact in the period 2011–12 just 13 out of 33 cases were upheld for disability discrimination (*Tribunals Statistics Quarterly* 2013), out of 100 registered appeals. (This can be compared with 3,600 appeals registered for SEN.)

The law is an imperfect device for dealing with the complexities of 'what's best for the child' when the driver of the decision-making is 'what's lawful' (King and King 2006). King and King, using the example of a tribunal for special educational needs, describe the way in which information is transformed (rather than simply transferred) as it is passed between institutions to enable legal decision-makers to reach a conclusion. Technical and expert information has to be selected, reduced and reconstructed to make decisions about what's right and wrong. Where health conditions or impairments are not static, rely for diagnosis on clusters of symptoms (such as chronic fatigue), are not predictable in their impact, issues of equity will be more challenging to a tribunal. Parents also have to provide tangible evidence that their child was discriminated against either because he is disabled or because he was perceived to be. Mediation is often acknowledged to be quicker and a way of avoiding the stress and expense of tribunals. Parents are not necessarily actively encouraged by local authorities to take this route (Riddell *et al.* 2010), although draft legislation now sets out a requirement for this to take place first. Arguably the real potential of the legislation lies in fostering a process that circumvents the need for a tribunal, encourages the two-way communication process that supports schools in knowing about the visible and invisible barriers that children encounter in participating in school activities and facilitates the development of appropriate supports. This book focuses on this constructive element.

Policy is of course enacted in different ways and settings by a range of actors. No longer can we conceive of policy being transmitted in a hierarchical way, some kind of governmental dictat that is uniformly rolled out. As Ball (2012) writes, 'Education policy is being "done" in new locations, on different scales, by new actors and organisations' (p. 4). Arguably this has always been true in some respects, including in the disability field. Global actors such as the World Health Organization, World Bank, OECD, Unicef and other United Nations bodies have all contributed to the developing disability landscape. Equally disability rights activists have been key players in shaping legislation in the UK and the government strategy document *Fulfilling Potential* (DWP 2013) welcomes the convening of a new cross-sector alliance by Disability Rights UK to influence the development of local services. However, Ball is pointing to the very interconnectedness of organizations and service providers, the mutuality and interdependence of the relationships that might at one time have been seen as hierarchical but are now characterized as rhizomatic networks, that develop narratives of what constitutes 'good policy' and practice. As local authorities in the UK publish the services that are available in their region for parents, the localized nature of these and their interconnectedness will become even more apparent. As policies move through these networks they are shaped and adapted by their diverse participants. This is even true when the driving force is legislation. Such requirements need translation. Education providers have to interpret what is particularly relevant to their setting just as case law has to be built over time. Policy responses are therefore situated within a local context, and while this book is focussed on enabling educationalists to be responsive and create environments where all children feel able to participate, it does not set out to be a rule book. As will become evident, the research that underpins the book and the development of resources were conceived as being adapted and tailored by participants according to their setting.

Politics and data collection

There is a power in having accurate statistics: they enable the framing of key issues for both a group as a whole and sub-groups within it, they allow the monitoring of current circumstances, as well as identifying changes and progress, they facilitate the evaluation of a policy or programme as well as supporting the forecasting of future needs and costs of policy changes. They are therefore a political tool, open to misuse as well as advocacy for positive change. The design of the tool is as much a factor as the way the data are analyzed and used. The decision of what data to collect and the phrasing of the questions shape the possibilities of how the data could be used. In a seminal article concerning the Office of Population Censuses and Surveys' collection of disability data, Abberley (1992), using the work of Oliver, illustrates the political nature of question wording illustrating how they reflect the model of disability and the oppressive nature of those which place the emphasis on an individual's limitations. For example, rather than asking:

Do you have a scar, blemish or deformity which limits your daily activities?

He suggests:

> Do other people's reactions to any scar, blemish or deformity you may
> have limit your daily activities?

He notes the political nature of the decision not to ask about defects in design
or access to equipment and the grave under-estimation of official figures,
especially with respect to the poverty experienced. This statement still has
resonance today with a media distinction between those unable or unwilling to
work, the deserving and the undeserving poor. Notably the Life Opportunities
Survey launched in 2009, designed to trace the experiences of disabled people
over time, includes items that seek to understand the reason for non-
participation in key life activities.

At the heart of the debate about how these data are collected lies unease at
collecting information that concerns the *experience* of a condition, rather than a
condition itself. Rather simplistically there has been a tendency to view data on
health conditions as objective data and that of experiences as subjective, as if the
former is in essence more valid than the latter. However, children receive diagnoses
of conditions with different degrees and types of assessment. This is particularly true
where the identification rests on the presence of clusters of symptoms, many of
which rely on self or other report. In practice neurological deficits are largely
inferred from profiles constructed on the basis of performance on psychological
tests or of reported accounts of behaviour in social settings. A study by Martin *et al.*
(2003) illustrates this well in their finding that 39 per cent of their sample of 75
autistic children had no standardized assessment prior to being statemented. Health
status may therefore be fluid, socially situated and as dynamic as experiential reports,
making 'objective' data different from subjective reports. It is this subjective element
that has been blamed for the difficulty of co-ordinating data management systems
between different aspects of social services (Lowson and Mahon 2009). Moreover
different services have traditionally required different information. Lowson and
Mahon describe how social care traditionally focuses on the broader functional
needs of a child, adopting a more holistic approach to enable them to live their lives
within the context of the family and community; whereas individual health services
address a narrower set of needs that relate to treating the underlying health condition
and alleviating symptoms. While education services collect data in relation to the
child's educational need, at the level of the school they may also hold some data
relating to health. Notably prior to the legislation none of these bodies required
information on whether or not the child was disabled as it had little relevance to
the provision of their service. However the introduction of disability discrimination
legislation has resulted in a requirement for all three services to identify those
children who are disabled. Guidance on the earlier DDA suggested that judgements
about the adverse effect of a health condition should be judged when the child was
six years or older. As education is a universal service for children over this age, there
are advantages to it taking the lead in the data collection process.

The context of the book

This book draws on a series of government research projects carried out by myself and colleagues (Harry Daniels, Jan Georgeson, Anthony Feiler, Jayne Hacker, Sue Martin, Debbie Watson and Beth Tarleton) designed to meet the challenges of collecting robust data on disability that could inform schools' responses to be proactive in making schools better places for learning for all children. The research was commissioned because of the government intention at that time to include disability as part of the Annual School Census.

No doubt one of the reasons why disability data had not been collected is because of the challenges they present. This issue will be pursued in more detail later. Perhaps at the outset however we can recognize that unlike other protected characteristics covered by the Equality Act, it requires the collection of subjective and experiential information about a condition that is not static. Thus while gender, age or pregnancy offer themselves up to professional expertise or validation, the same is not easily stated with respect to disability. The Code of Practice in relation to the 1995 Act clearly stated an expectation on schools to collect disability data:

> 7.8 It may not be immediately obvious that a child is disabled. Underachievement and difficult behaviour may, in some cases, indicate an underlying disability which has not yet been identified. A responsible body may have difficulty claiming not to have known about a disability if, on the basis of such indicators, it might reasonably have been expected to have known that a pupil was disabled.
> 7.9 It will be in the interests of responsible bodies to ensure that schools are proactive in seeking out information. If they are not, the responsible body may not be able to claim lack of knowledge about a pupil's disability.

The guidance fostered awareness of the sensitivity of these data.

> In seeking out information responsible bodies may, for example:
> want to establish an atmosphere and culture at the school which is open and welcoming, so that pupils and parents feel comfortable about disclosing information about a disability; ask parents, when they visit or during the admissions process, about the existence of and the nature of any disability that their child may have; provide continuing opportunities to share information, for example when seeking permission to go on a school trip or at points of transition within the school.
>
> (DRC 2002)

At the time of writing there are no similar clear statements following the Equality Act.

At the time the work was commissioned the data were to inform school returns to the annual census, enabling local authorities and the government to monitor the impact of their policies and practices on disabled children. A dual approach was taken to collecting these data. Parents were asked to complete a questionnaire that would include information about what their child found particularly helpful. Additionally, at the outset of the project, despite government caution in relation to the age of the child, a firm decision was made that *all* children should be given the opportunity and means to contribute their experiences on the barriers and supports to learning and that they would also be asked about the experience of disability. This approach was consistent with the subsequent recommendation and spirit of the WHO/World Bank 2011 report, marking the 'moral duty to remove the barriers to participation', placing the experience of an impairment at the heart of the data collection process. Within the report there is a priority recommendation to 'consult and involve children in decisions about their education' (p. 227). The voices of disabled people are central to the rights agenda, setting a moral imperative to privilege their views.

The parent questionnaire and activities to capture children's views were developed, trialled and then further tested across 50 local authorities and over 100 schools. In total we surveyed 16,000 pupils across the country. In the following chapters the studies are referred to as:

- phase 1, the development, piloting and trialling phase;
- phase 2, testing the utility and use of the tools by schools.

A universal approach was adopted across both phases to ensure that the tools were successful in helping schools to learn about children who had largely hidden the impact of their condition. We also included special schools as although they have typically closer contact with parents, they do not necessarily collect data that could help them to identify barriers within their particular environment.

Government-funded projects are developed within a particular time frame for reporting and often commissioned in stages. The book therefore provides an opportunity to examine in greater depth the data we collected, drawing together the data from the phases and where appropriate carry out further analysis. The work can also be embedded more fully within the context of recent literature and issues raised that were outside our direct remit at that time.

Conclusion

This chapter has set out the context for addressing the book's two prime aims. First, as stated at the outset, it aims to increase policy-makers' understanding of the term disability and second to enable them to respond proactively to remove organizational practices that disadvantage and marginalize disabled children. Attention has been drawn to the way in which disabled children are clearly disadvantaged across a number of important measures that determine their wellbeing. Their marginalization has been recognized both nationally and internationally. The driver for change has been a rights agenda and the introduction of legislation to safeguard their rights. In many ways the law is an imperfect tool and its effectiveness is limited by a number of factors:

- A widespread lack of understanding of the term and confusion with special educational needs.
- Inequitable knowledge and understanding of the law as a means of upholding rights.
- The law being a cumbersome and complex tool for bringing about change.
- The rhizomatic way in which policies and practices now operate lead to varied and multiple understandings of disability and use of the term.
- The compounding of these limitations by the lack of a consensus concerning the collection of disability data.

If schools, local authorities and central government don't know who the disabled are, we are unable to safeguard their rights, children will continue to be discriminated against, to 'slip through the net' of provision and be open to abuse and neglect.

The book interweaves three elements: a conceptual understanding of disability – to provide a clear value-driven framework for professional responses; an empirical illustration of the development of materials to support an understanding of why the process of disability data collection cannot simply be reduced to two questions on a form; and some embedded illustrative case study material to provide exemplars of how the materials can be contextualized and used to make adjustments to enhance the participation of all children.

In the next chapter contrasting approaches to understanding disability in childhood will be presented to provide the important conceptual underpinning to the development of disability data collection tools. The social models of disability will be explored, understanding the nature of oppression, together with the tensions that exist in ignoring impairment, emphasizing sameness and making disability the central identifier. The provision of the biopsychosocial model that underpins the World Health Organization approach to disability will be examined, and the limits of providing a culture free tool for collecting disability data. Extensions to the social model, the interactional and relational model have highlighted the ways in which individual and social elements have combined and provided insights into the way in which external oppression is compounded by being internalized. Finally the capability approach on which much of the United Nations approach is based will be examined. The chapter will conclude by drawing together the principles that underpinned the development of the disability data collection tools.

Having set the scene in relation to values the focus in Chapter 3 will be on the technical considerations in developing methods to gather data on disability.

This chapter will draw on previous research to consider key issues in the language and phrasing of questions around physical and mental health conditions, impairments and diagnoses; the development of questions that address the experience of barriers and supports, of impact in relation to the restriction or limitation on participation, as well as functioning. These issues are placed within the content of the purpose of the Equality Act. The findings of the survey will be used to illustrate the importance of using multiple indicators, the ways in which measures of impact refine estimates of those children who meet the Equality Act criteria and the relationship between impact and need. The findings highlight the dangers of using SEN as a proxy measure and equating functioning with impact.

In Chapter 4 qualitative data from the parent questionnaire are analyzed to understand what parents consider to be particularly supportive for their child. Access to adults featured heavily in parental responses, with a quarter specifically referring to individual support, small groups or small classes, and most often to simply refer to a teaching assistant. Parents saw this form of organization as essential for the child's learning, in sharp contrast to recent research that questions the use of teaching assistants. This requirement was often linked in parent comments to providing a positive emotional climate, one where staff gave encouragement and reassurance. In secondary schools there was a slight shift in parental responses to focus on the nature of the relationships children have with adults, whether they are understanding and supportive in their attitude towards the child. Notably this was also cited as an aspect that created barriers for their child. The needs of different groups are also considered, drawing out responses from parents of children with autism spectrum disorder (ASD), asthma and mental health difficulties, three conditions which are increasing in prevalence. These groups reflect both general needs for understanding, as well as individual and often flexible school responses.

We turn then, in Chapter 5, to consider what children say, following a brief overview of issues in collecting children's views to set the scene. This chapter provides examples of the tools that schools used and how they adapted them to collect information from children about the barriers and supports to participation. In many instances schools shared their raw data with us, providing a unique opportunity to look at a wide-ranging group of young people from over 40 schools and examine whether there were any reoccurring themes, any shared meaning to attach to the nature of barriers and supports for disabled children. The data suggested that it was the social aspects of schooling that particularly impinge on children, and that these often (but not always) concern the informal aspects of school life. These involve the times and spaces/places of the school that make children feel best but that can also be most troubling. In secondary school the data on barriers to participation focus on relationships, interactions with peers and those with teachers. Whereas in primary school pupils look to both friends and teachers for support, it is the former that are key to survival. The pupils' views contrast to those of parents who focus on the presence of adults to support their child, rarely mentioning the importance of friends. Finally the chapter reflects on the strengths and limitations of the different tools, recognizing the value of looking within and across the data, to hear both individual and collective voices.

Chapter 6 focuses on what schools learned from the data, what they found useful and how they responded. The chapter draws on interviews with professionals in schools and local authorities together with observations of children in class. It explores data that indicate discrepancies between that information provided by parents and the views within an organization. Overall the data suggest that schools are mainly aware of difficulties that give rise to problems with participating in class lessons, but not when the difficulties were experienced elsewhere. The parental questionnaire therefore surfaced difficulties that remain invisible to the school and have hitherto been unreported. This draws attention to the invisibility of some of the challenges children face and the importance for schools in collecting these data. Finally the use of the data to monitor achievement in pupils is illustrated, again drawing attention to those children who may escape the notice of the school as they meet age-related expectations even though they have the potential for higher achievement.

The final chapter, Chapter 7, draws together the findings of the research to consider the implications both in relation to school policy and practices and in the wider context of collecting disability data. It revisits the place of a rights-based approach and argues that, despite the challenges, schools are better placed to engage with the meaning of disability through meeting their disability equality duties. In consequence they gain a better understanding of the nature of disabling experiences and are enabled to respond proactively to offset these. These understandings are set within the overwhelming view of children of schools as social institutions. The collection of disability data enables schools to go beyond the rhetoric laid down in plans and schemes and provide evidence that they are meeting the needs of all children. It establishes the need to go further than recognizing the need for individual adjustments and develop a culture that actively supports all children to recognize and think critically about disempowering discourses as they relate to all protected characteristics – bringing to the fore that disability is a public rather than an individual issue. This chapter also explores the wider implications of our research for the way that data are collected. Our approach to the collection revealed important gaps in current practice – not least the disconnect between disability and special educational needs, and the limitations of using the latter as a single proxy measure. The data revealed the pivotal role of impact in understanding disability and contribute further evidence for understanding that disability is contextually and culturally situated, and can only be understood and responded to in that light. Equity like inclusion is not an end state. Schools play a vital role in enabling young people to have the freedom to choose to live the life that they value.

Chapter 2

Understanding disability

Introduction

The driver of the research on disability data collection was the Disability Discrimination Act 1995 and subsequent Equality Act 2010. Legislation has introduced a set of defining criteria for disability, however this needs to be seen in relation to the purpose of the research – developing a tool for making judicial decisions in relation to discrimination. The set of three key elements (impairment, functioning, impact) contribute to a broader understanding of disability, depending on how they are acted on. They don't provide the guiding set of values needed to underpin decision-making in relation to services. Children's impairments and health conditions may be identified and responded to, but in a manner that is not empowering for the pupil. It is therefore important that organizations have a shared understanding of disability, a conceptual framework from which to interrogate proposed policies and practices, a reference point from which to monitor and evaluate the outcomes. To inform this we need to engage with a more scholarly and political literature and unpick the debates in this complex and sometimes bitterly contested area. Writers come from a number of fields – disability studies, philosophy of education, medical sociology – each with a distinct approach to the area. They provide a number of different perspectives through which to understand disability but largely with reference to adults, much less attention is given to children. Conversely, those focussing on children direct their attention to the organization of schooling, the site of possible segregation and exclusion, and the meanings of inclusion. For most writers, the one area of agreement lies with profound dissatisfaction with the medical model – an approach that portrays disability simply in terms of impairment, a deficit that resides within the individual, a tragedy that requires medical treatment and rehabilitation, most usually by way of segregated services and institutions, effectively removing the person from an ordinary everyday life.

This chapter presents contrasting approaches to understanding disability, drawing on the adult literature to reflect on childhood and the implications of these models for the ways in which education systems respond. It is a broad and wide-ranging literature and what is presented here is an overview, at times of necessity reductive. It provides however a starting point to support the reader in adopting a series of different lenses through which to begin to understand disability. These take the form of different models (social, biopsychosocial, social relational and interactional). They provide important ways of seeing disability, but as Waddell and Aylward (2010) suggest, they should not be adopted uncritically. Rather they serve here as a tool that we use in an eclectic manner to inform and underpin the development of the disability data collection methods. What starts as a quest for understanding disability becomes a journey to understanding sources of inequality – what the Equality Act seeks to redress. I therefore examine the implications of these models with respect to policy and practice for children, placed within the context of equalization of opportunity and here capability theory provides a useful tool. The chapter will conclude by drawing together a number of core principles that guided the development of the research tools. These reflect the challenge of providing the means to surface subjective experiences that will inform school practices, while also providing data that can be aggregated to steer wider policy developments.

Understanding disability from the perspective of the social model

One of the most influential drivers of change has been the introduction and adoption of what has been termed 'the social model'. It has influenced the work of the European Community, and the United Nations resulting in the UN Convention on the Rights for Disabled People. It has of course had significant impact in the UK. The model was adopted by the Disability Rights Commission, set up in 2000, and underpins the government paper on *Improving the Life Chances of Disabled People* published in 2005. It underpins the work of the Office for Disability Issues set up in 2005 (as part of the Department for Work and Pensions) to work across all areas of government policy to enable disabled people to be fully participating members of society. Its website provides a user-friendly definition of the social model, namely that 'disability is created by barriers in society' and provides three categories – environmental, attitudinal and organizational barriers. This 'easy to access' definition steers away from a discussion of the place of impairment, of material disadvantage or oppression, rather it alludes to the solution: 'the removal of these barriers within society, or the reduction of their effects, rather than trying to fix an individual's impairment or health condition'. As we will see there are different positions that fall broadly within the social model that provide insights into the nature of the barriers encountered.

The origins of the social model lie with Finkelstein, the founding father who, together with Paul Hunt, set up the Union of the Physically Impaired Against Segregation in 1972, as a resistance movement against oppression. The purpose was to home in on the way in which society worked, identifying the competitive market as a bar to disabled people's emancipation. Finkelstein (2001) sets out the basic tenet: 'It is society that disables us and disabled people are an oppressed social group'. He continues: 'our society is constructed *by* people with capabilities *for* people with capabilities and it is *this* that makes people with impairments incapable of functioning' (p. 2).

Finkelstein refers to the approach as an 'interpretation of the *nature* of disability' (p. 1) rather than an explanatory model as disabled people were not the subject. The focus was the discriminatory practices of society. As Barnes (2012) later explains this perspective does not set out to deny that interventions directed at the individual are of value but they fail to empower disabled people. Instead attention is shifted from functional limitations onto 'the problems caused by disabling environments, barriers and cultures'.

The social approach was elaborated by Oliver, a sociologist, who introduced the term social model (1983). This first wave of the social model emphasized economic and materialist disadvantages. As a sociologist, Oliver drew on a Marxist tradition, locating disability historically within the rise of capitalism. His focus lay with material inequalities, arising from economic and employment disparities. The real issues for him were 'oppression, discrimination, inequality and poverty' (Oliver 1990). This firmly placed the rise of the social model as an expression of political activism. Abberley (1987), another key writer of the time, argued that disabled people were lower paid, had poorer working conditions and were more likely to be unemployed. Oppression was also manifest in the distorted and stereotyped image of the disabled person and these two sources served to maintain the existing structure of work and social organization. A key element of the social model has therefore been its emancipatory purpose and political function, a matter for policy at every level.

Oliver (2004) provides useful examples of what the social model might mean in policy terms, in what he refers to as a *citizenship approach*, where equal and full rights and responsibilities are accorded with respect to economic, political and moral dimensions. Disabled people are seen as a powerful interest group in the development of services, active citizens contributing as valued workers and consumers. He contrasts this to humanitarian policies and provision, driven by goodwill and a desire to help, but the services are controlled by others who may think they are doing 'a good job', but lacking the active involvement of disabled people in decision-making, the services fail to match the needs of disabled people. He identifies a third approach, the compliance approach, which is particularly pertinent here, as it is driven by legislation and government policy. He notes the dangers of policies and practices established and evaluated by the extent to which they meet the required minimum basic standards.

The social model therefore places an emphasis on policies that promote participation and empowerment to bring about environmental and organizational transformations. If we apply this to childhood, it is schools therefore that are the focus of change rather than the individual child. As we shall see later, there are strong implications that the approach should be one where schools cater for the diversity of children, where the process of education is inclusive rather than serving to exclude and segregate.

Criticisms and extensions to the social model

The social model has spawned a series of debates about the adequacy of its explanatory powers, of its naivety in ignoring impairment, and of its singular focus on disability as an identifier. These aspects will be examined in turn as they serve to highlight the complexity of the field and provide important insights that guide us further in developing an approach to disability data collection.

One frequent criticism of the social model lies with the limited way in which it has been used to *explain* the ways in which societal barriers lead to disability. In part this has led to discussion about the meaning of the term 'model'. Notably, as we have seen, Finkelstein uses the term 'approach' and Oliver refers to it as 'a practical tool, not a theory, an idea or a concept' (2004, pp. 18–31), one that can directly inform policy and practice. Finkelstein (2004) reminds us that:

> Models are constructed so that an object can be looked at in different ways and under different conditions. A good model can enable us to see something which we do not understand because in the model it can be seen from different viewpoints (not available to us in reality) and it is this multi-dimensioned replica of reality that can trigger insights which we might not otherwise develop.
>
> (p. 16)

Although writers refer to 'the social model' there, there was no intention to provide an underlying theory or explanations of how 'it' works; rather, as Thomas (2004) refers to, its origin served as a rallying cry, designed to unite disabled people in a crusade for change and draw public awareness to the rights of this marginalized group.

The cost of placing emphasis on collective solidarity and social change was that the experience of an individual's impairments was deemed private and personal (Oliver 1996) and this has become the focus of much debate in the area. Concerns have been raised that it focused on a particular group of disabled people, even when the approach was widened from its origins of a union of people with a physical impairment. It failed to represent mental health service users or people with intellectual disabilities or autism, leading some to perceive this as indicating hierarchies of impairment, implying one model for one group and another for others (Reeve 2012; Shakespeare 2006). Accusations have been made that denial of the experience of impairment was disempowering (Shakespeare 2006). It failed to address conditions that were progressive or cyclical. While some disabled people enjoy good health others experience pain, fatigue, vertigo. These experiences are not necessarily static, they can impact both on a regular and irregular basis. As Rhodes *et al.* (2008) argue with respect to epilepsy an all-or-nothing approach is simply not appropriate.

Closs (2000) illustrates this further in relation to health conditions in children where many will fall within a grey area, not really well nor ill. There is therefore a fluidity to the experience of impairment which critics felt was not addressed through the social model. Goodley and Roets (2008) go further still in describing impairment as a 'mobile and moving set of differences' (p. 250). They argue that there is a need to problematize the notion of impairment.

Despite these criticisms and concerns the social model has spawned a variety of approaches to understanding disability which, to differing degrees, build on and extend its basic tenets and it is to these I now turn.

Biopsychosocial approaches

The response by the medical field has been to incorporate social aspects, going beyond a simple disease and functioning model. Waddell and Aylward (2010) distinguish between impairment, presence of a medical condition and experience, although notably also illustrate how diagnoses rest on the reporting of the patient's experience. Impairment is a medical term – it provides 'the most objective measure of a health condition' but not about the experience. Waddell and Aylward point to the inadequacy of medical models to explain why people with the same condition respond very differently. While a condition may determine the boundaries of capacity it doesn't determine performance. They advocate a model which takes into account a wide range of personal and subjective experiences, including:

- assumptions, perceptions and expectations (by the individual, family, health professionals and employers, which may interact and reinforce each other);
- attitudes and beliefs, emotions, moods, values, goals, expectations, psychological distress and coping strategies;
- motivation and effort;
- uncertainty, anxiety and fear avoidance;
- depression.

Waddell and Aylward (2010) argue that the medical model is particularly problematic for mental illness, as a 'disease model' ignores socio-cultural and psychological factors. Moreover:

it does not include the patient or their unique human attributes and subjective experience ... [instead] The patient's reports of illness are reduced to a set of symptoms and signs of disease ... critics argue that the medical model is simplistic, incorrectly assumes that all illness has a single cause ... and fails to take account of the personal and social dimensions of sickness and disability.

(p. 11)

Notably it is still driven by an individualistic explanation of disability.

These views are ones shared by the World Health Organization. In the most recent *World Report on Disability* (WHO and World Bank 2011) the argument is set out in the opening chapter that:

> The medical model and the social model are often presented as dichotomous, but disability should be viewed neither as purely medical nor as purely social: persons with disabilities can often experience problems arising from their health condition. A balanced approach is needed, giving appropriate weight to the different aspects of disability.

(p. 4)

This approach underpins the International Classification of Functioning (ICF) coding framework that charts the interaction between body functions/structures, activity and participation and environmental factors (WHO 2001). This was later extended to children and youth (ICF-CY; WHO 2007). It is designed as a 'scientific' tool with an emphasis on objective measures rather than subjective experience (Coster and Khetani 2008). It therefore has limitations with respect to including what are personally relevant and meaningful activities and to considering whether an experience may be satisfying, thereby risking equating quantity with quality (Coster and Khetani 2008). In aiming to develop a cross-cultural tool, it has to de-contextualize, and remove culturally relevant activities.

Set alongside these limitations are a number of important strengths. The WHO approach recognizes that disability is 'a universal feature of the human condition'. It is not a fixed entity but fluid, continuous and the whole population is 'at risk' at some point in their lives. The *World Report* states that the experience of inequality does not always fit into the 'mould of discrimination' (WHO and World Bank 2011). Instead, what is needed is recognition of distributive injustices as people are denied opportunities and resources. Globally, those who fare worse are those with the most complex needs.

As we will see, this biopsychosocial approach has some aspects in common with relational approaches in that it understands disability 'against the backdrop of a relationship between individual and contextual factors' (Gustavvson *et al.* 2005, p. 34). However, the WHO framework does not provide an analysis of the interaction between the elements of functioning, activity and participation. It is essentially an individual model with the starting point being the presence of a disease and the restrictions and limitations that disadvantage a person as a result. There is no account of the experience of oppression. The foregrounding of 'bio' makes it unacceptable to many disability scholars.

The prominence of the individual impairment in the biopsychosocial model is mirrored in legislation, opening it up to the same criticisms of reducing the experience of impairment to measures of functioning and access to generic rather than personally valued activities and ways of participating. It is important therefore to see how these limitations can be offset and look at how others have developed the social model.

Relational and interactive models

Reindal (2010b) makes a helpful distinction, in setting out his adoption of a social relational model, helping us to understand the differences with a biopsychosocial approach. Like others he argues that it is absurd to consider that disability is only caused by social barriers but that a distinction can be made between the conditions that are necessary for disability (i.e. an impairment effect) and those which are sufficient. Impairment effect on its own is a necessary element of disability but not sufficient as a cause, to be understood one needs to look at both social and personal implications. He argues that the impairment effect on its own 'is not equivalent to the *state of being disabled*. Disability is something *imposed on top* of the impairment effect, due to ideological, social and environmental consequences' (p. 130).

Watson (2004) also critiques the social model for its rejection of experience and consequently its failure to portray the complexity and diversity of people's lives. He argues that it too readily accepts the duality of disabled/non-disabled – failing to recognize that many do not identify with the term. Indeed he argues that it ignores people who wish to be ordinary, not activists, nor a separate social group. In doing so it denies the individuality of people, obscuring the diversity that lies within the group. More controversially he also argues that there can be no barrier-free environment as removing obstacles for some can exclude others. People with impairment would not necessarily be included even if we manage to remove barriers. Watson (2004) argues that it is the 'withholding of social and cultural recognition' rather than 'competing for scarce resources' that contributes to the experience of disablement.

Like Watson and Reindal, a number of other writers have also pointed to the naivety of removing environmental barriers as the source of oppression. French (1993), for example, describes how her visual impairment makes it hard to recognize people and when the sun comes out it is challenging to read non-verbal cues, or in turn to emit her own. She tried to manage this situation when she moved house by warning new neighbours that she might well walk by without greeting them but this strategy was only partially successful. Interactions were still strained as when neighbours did speak to her she was 'jolted abruptly from her thoughts' and consequently often did not respond normally. She argues that such impairments are not easily eradicated through manipulating the environment. The complex interaction, between the individual, the impairment and the environment, are also well illustrated by

Richard Rieser (1990), writing about his childhood experience of contracting polio and undergoing extensive treatment to enable him to walk without a calliper or stick:

> My memories of my younger childhood were of pain from my treatment and forcing myself to do all sorts of things … Physically I could do a great many things, but my personality was less resilient to growing up disabled … I recollect when I was occasionally to glimpse my lopsided gait in shop windows, not believing it was me, but at the same time knowing it was and being shocked and depressed.
>
> (p. 29)

His account of schooling illustrates the ways in which his interaction with his peers and others contribute to his identity (p. 29):

> The need to be tough, to cope, to be what is now called a super-cripple left no space for sensitive feelings and 'soft' creativity … In one way they treated me as if I was just the same as all the others and I suppose that was why I like it. The problem was I wasn't just the same!

These two accounts are a reminder of the centrality of hearing first-hand about the experiences of a disabled child.

Adopting a social relational model, Thomas (2004), like Rieser and French, emphasizes the way in which social relationships operate between the 'impaired' and the 'non-impaired', the impact and effect of social behaviour, but also noting the effects on people's sense of self and self-esteem. Thomas (2004) describes how 'disability involves a nexus of relationships between those designated impaired and those designated non-impaired … relationships that work to exclude and disadvantage the former while promoting the relative inclusion and privileging of the latter' (p. 33).

These experiences reveal the complexities of managing an impairment and have led writers to coin the term internalized oppression to describe the psycho-emotional impact, not to replace the social model but to demonstrate how they are experienced jointly with external oppression. Reeve (2012) describes the two-fold way in which internalized oppression can operate, first in a direct way in the interactions between disabled and non-disabled people and second in an indirect way through internalizing the prejudices and attitudes of others. She gives examples of the reaction of strangers, avoiding interactions with her or asking what's wrong, as direct oppression, leading to uncertainty about how the next stranger will react, calling in effect for her to manage the situation. She writes that 'one of the difficulties facing disabled people within social interactions is that there is a lack of culturally agreed rules of engagement' (p. 81). This leads to fear of doing the wrong thing. Using the term 'internalized ableism' Reeve writes about adopting the norms and behaviours of the able-bodied as a form of indirect psycho-emotional disablism. She links internalized oppression with structural aspects describing how barriers within the environment, such as inaccessible spaces, impact on one's sense of self: 'you are out of place, you are different' (p. 82), a reminder of the physicality of our bodies, something that is forgotten until it causes a problem. Where the impairment is invisible there is constant management of what to disclose and to whom, and awareness that you may not be believed. Reeve (2012) writes about how difficult it is to challenge this form of oppression as everyday interactions, images, aesthetic judgements and evaluations, jokes, indeed the way that ableism is endemic within society, contribute to internalized oppression.

Shakespeare (1996) describes the process as one where identity is shaped from above by schools and other agencies as well as from the self and 'the stories we tell ourselves' in finding a way through. He also however raises another central objection to the social model – the assumption that disability is at the core of an identity, ignoring the choices that people make and the multiple layers of identity. Research by Watson (1999) draws attention to the fluidity with which some 11–16-year-olds see themselves as disabled in one context and not in another, and in later research adults who do not see themselves as disabled in that their identity is not based around their impairment.

These descriptions illustrate how writers on the one hand critique the social model but on the other incorporate important and key elements in their account, extending our understanding rather than denying its relevance. They do however indicate an important way in which societal values contribute to an internalized oppression. Indeed through extending and incorporating additional cultural meanings they draw attention to the importance of language, discourse and the media and how these are then played out in everyday interactions. If we examine this literature in the context of models of disability we can start to appreciate the important role that schools play in mediating these social messages.

Disability and cultural values

As society has become increasingly health-conscious, there has been greater public awareness on the body, and having a body that does not conform to the Western standard of 'lean strong and physically fit' (Riddell and Watson 2003, p. 8) is seen as a failure to take regular exercise, eat an appropriate diet, to demonstrate self-discipline, rather than due to misfortune. In a health-conscious society, one's body is central to identity and the way others see you. As one of the participants in a study by Peuravaara (2013) says, 'It's the superficial surface that makes you memorable'. Shakespeare (1994) goes further to argue for the importance of recognizing the 'ethic of invincibility or perfectibility' in cultural representations of disability:

It is not just that disabled people are different, expensive, inconvenient, or odd: it is that they represent a threat – either ... to order, or, to the self-conception of western human beings – who, since the Enlightenment, have viewed themselves as perfectible, as all-knowing, as godlike: able, over and above all other beings, to conquer the limitations of their nature through the victories of their culture

(p. 298)

It is significant that the event that has developed most public awareness of disability in the UK was the Paralympics, which in 2012 had a record 11.4 million people viewing the opening ceremony. Disabled people appeared in living rooms around the country for the first time, demonstrating considerable physical achievements and challenging negative perceptions of incompetence (Smith and Sparkes 2012). As Williams (2012), writing in the *Guardian* following the games, suggests, the expectations were high and there is a common view that they were exceeded: 'Our mission was to create a public that is at ease and comfortable with disability and I think we've achieved that. An able-bodied person is never going to look at a disabled person the same way ever again ... Everybody who has watched the Paralympics has been changed by what they have witnessed.' However while this event can be individually empowering, it does however perpetuate a medicalized understanding of disability. Notably the word 'disability' is used interchangeably with 'impairment'. Athletes are carefully categorized and classified in relation to their impairments in a manner that is rarely seen outside the sporting arena. An understanding of the classification system is essential to understanding the format of the competition.

Smith and Sparkes (2012) describe how the media perpetuate stereotypes through depicting disabled athletes 'as victims or courageous individuals who battle against the odds and overcome their tragic disabled fate' and 'foster unrealistic expectations about what disabled people can achieve, or what they *should* achieve, if only they tried hard enough ... that all is needed when one is impaired is heroic individual effort and inner drive to overcome societal barriers' (p. 338). Cohen-Rottenberg (2012) echoes these sentiments: 'disability is a sign of utter helplessness that only a hero can overcome. Moreover, disabled people must rise to the level of heroism in order to be considered of worth.' At an individual level athletes cite a number of personal benefits including significant social affirmation, raised self-confidence and self-esteem and bodily mastery. They can also be inspirational, challenging low expectations and assumptions about functional limitations, notions of the body as fixed and static. These divergent views illustrate the complexity for schools in developing a culture which empowers rather than oppresses. Simple awareness-raising can fall far short of what is required to develop the culture of the school. A small-scale study by Fitzgerald (2012) of non-disabled 11–12-year-olds suggests that mere exposure can perpetuate deficit views of disability and indicate the importance of raising awareness of structural, cultural and economic constructions of disability. A core theme that emerged in the children's discussion around disability sport was one of difference and while not uniform the predominant view of the young people was summed up by one as 'It's not normal to be like that, pretty sad', with a distancing of the young people from both the athletes and their sports. Fitzgerald argues for the importance of young people engaging in disability sports, not simply to satisfy their curiosity but in order to move beyond their deficit-laden conceptions. The data provide a salutary reminder of the significant role schools have yet to play and yet we also know from research by Beckett and Buckner (2012) that schools are often fearful of 'getting it wrong' and lack the resources to be proactive in enabling pupils to engage critically with the ways in which society disables.

Implications for schools

When approaches to understanding disability are brought to bear on schools as organizations there are complex factors at work. Changes to the curriculum, testing, inspection and standards, and league tables all impact on schools' willingness and capacity to respond to the diversity of children. As Moore and Slee (2012) argue, these factors can lead schools to identify increasing numbers of children who lower the rankings, children that are seen to fit better elsewhere. As they state, 'policy enables and disables; it allocates those who have values and those who are invalids' (p. 229). As countries judge their children's achievements against one another and schools compare their position to others, the race to improve test scores produces increasing numbers of casualties – the social model provides an important vehicle for understanding disadvantage and oppression in schooling.

The term inclusive schooling, introduced to describe schools that provide for *all* children, has been adopted on a wide scale but refers to many contrasting practices. Thus inclusion can be used to describe disabled children located within mainstream education, yet receiving separate provision, to classes where provision is differentiated for individual needs, and schools where the curriculum, organization for learning and pedagogy reflect the diversity of individuals – what has also been referred to as Education For All (Ainscow 2007). Others have argued that the widespread adoption of the term inclusive education in fact means providing for children with special educational needs, i.e. special education (Moore and Slee 2012). 'Inclusive' schools therefore continue to locate the 'problem' to the child, rather than focussing on organizational, pedagogic and curriculum barriers. Ainscow (2007) outlines a working definition of inclusion with four key elements:

1 A process whereby there is 'a never ending search to find better ways of responding to diversity'.
2 The 'identification and removal of barriers'.

3   This involves 'collecting, collating and evaluating information from a wide range of sources in order to plan for improvements in policy and practice'.
4   It is 'about the presence, participation and achievement of all students'.

(pp. 155–156)

These elements are highly compatible with the approach adopted in developing the disability tools. However that is not to ignore the place of special schools for collecting these data, children can be marginalized and discriminated against in all types of school. For disability theorists there is a clear connection between place and belonging. Different social environments provide different affordances for the relationships we make with others. These in turn contribute to the construction of our identities; the way we view ourselves is intimately entwined with how we view our surroundings, and our sense of place in the world. It's not therefore solely about school but how these identities and roles are challenged across the borders between school and home and the community. Different settings call on different capabilities and there is an additional way of understanding sources of inequality. As we will see capability theory helps schools respond in a manner that doesn't interpret difference as 'deviance from normality or the postmodern celebration of difference that comes perilously close to ignoring the difficulties that pupils with impairments experience' (Reindal 2010a, p. 4). The discussion put forward by the capability approach emphasizes ends rather than means thereby moving away from the polarity of debates around specialist provision, curriculum and pedagogy or education for all.

Capability approach

The capability approach was developed by Amartya Sen, a Nobel prize winning economist, and Martha Nussbaum, an American professor of philosophy and law. Its origin lies in welfare economics. It provides a way to analyze wellbeing and standards of living but it has been explored in relation to disability to provide an understanding of difference that is not understood in relation to some notions of the norm. As Terzi (2007) describes, disability can be conceptualized in relation to capabilities, and by this she means people's freedom to achieve their own wellbeing, opportunities to choose (or indeed not) what they can do or become. This is proposed as the real source of inequality or equality, shifting the focus away from individual or social understandings of disability. Capability is understood as a 'practical opportunity' (Mitra 2006) and the second core concept is that of 'functioning', the *achievement through being and doing*. The emphasis lies with the outcome (rather than the cause) – differential treatment in order to have equally 'effective opportunities and access to ... basic functionings' that are 'essential pre-requisites for an equal participation in society' (Terzi 2007, p. 758). The analogy that is often used is the freedom of Gandhi to fast as compared with those experiencing a famine.

Human agency is therefore at the heart. As Reindal (2010a) states, 'the capability perspective transforms the understanding of disability as a natural condition caused by an impairment into an issue intimately related to social and environmental inequalities, which restrict freedoms and opportunities' (p. 6). In this sense it is consistent with a social model in identifying barriers and discrimination. The approach is highly compatible with a Rights model in that the focus is on equal access. Terzi (2008) expresses how:

> we can think of impairment and disability as aspects of human diversity … This allows for a conceptualization of disability as emerging precisely from the interlocking of … personal, social and circumstantial factors … Impairment … is a personal feature that becomes an disability – an inability to perform some significant class of functionings on average performed by someone's reference group under common circumstances – when it interacts with specific social and environmental structures. Disability is, therefore relational both with respect to impairment and to the design of social institutions.
>
> (Terzi 2008, p. 251)

Seeing disability as one aspect of the heterogenity of humans is fundamental to overcoming discrimination and oppression. Resourcing (environmental setting, policies, physical and human resources) is determined by equal access to fundamental educational functionings 'like being able to read and write, or to concentrate and accomplish tasks, or to reflect critically on one's own actions' (Terzi 2007, p. 762). The role of school is therefore to provide the conditions for the functioning to be achieved: 'transformational resources that will allow them to choose the kind of life they have reason to value' (Terzi 2007, p. 765), the limits being set by what is 'necessary to the individual's effective participation'.

The capability approach recognizes the varied ways in which impairment impacts on daily life. Mitra (2006) distinguishes between potential and actual disability:

> The onset of a severe physical or mental impairment will almost inevitably lead to a reduction in the range of an individual's practical opportunities … in the capability set, and thus to potential disability … Whether the individual is actually disabled depends on whether the impairment places restrictions on the individual functionings … what an individual values doing (or being) and on what the individual succeeds in doing/being.
>
> (Mitra 2006, p. 241)

This reinforces an understanding of disability as dynamic and discontinuous.

As Florian et al. (2008) argue, the capability approach, although under-developed with respect to education, provides a different conceptual lens through which to view educational provision, not seeking to understand people in relation to how they differ, but in relation to the difference between their capability to choose and achieve different functions. It is not argued here however that it provides a sole lens. There is an element that is more forcefully conveyed of the relational, interactive and affective dimension through a model that is not derived through economics and resources.

In summary

The social model has been hugely influential in bringing to the fore the discriminatory practices in society with a strong argument that responses need to be empowering and promote participation. Watson (2012) has stressed the importance of also seeing children as active agents, adopting an approach that reflects their perspective of what is most important in bringing quality to their life. This is an important reminder that too often we take our cue from parents or professionals. We need an approach that reflects the fact that these priorities may change over time – perhaps because the child is developing and maturing or perhaps because the impairment changes. This calls on us to recognize the barriers and supports to participation and the ways in which these may change over time. These tenets are strong and powerful values on which to build a responsive system and against which to evaluate the success of our endeavours. The biopsychosocial response of the World Health Organization was to emphasize the universality of disability yet without undermining the place of the individual. The ICF tools identify disability using a coding system that strives to produce objective and comparable measures where functioning is measured alongside activity and participation, and does so within a context-free system. However the particular values that infuse a person's experience are undermined. Reindal (2010b) has drawn attention to the importance of recognizing the impact over and above an impairment effect which the ICF framework does not really address. The relational social model provides a lens to understand the dual way in which oppression occurs, and the interaction between external and internal sources of oppression. This challenges us to look more closely at the ways these messages are conveyed both through the media and more locally in schools and other organizations. Finally we have drawn on capability theory to reinforce the importance of understanding sources of inequality and that these lie in access to resources and support for people's freedom to choose what they want to do and become, including in a school context access to the basket of skills that support their success in what they value doing and becoming.

Implications and messages for disability data collection

This chapter has presented a number of different models that scholars and activists have developed for understanding disability. For our purposes the task is to consider the implications for approaches to disability data collection, teasing out the complexities between commonly used terms such as impairment, functioning and disability and in particular set what are often seen as technical challenges within a conceptual framework. A particular aim is to respond to legislation in a way that promotes social justice and counters simple compliance and performativity. Rather than simply weighing up the strengths and limitations of each model I have drawn eclectically from them, mindful that in doing that there will be conflicting forces at work, tensions to be acknowledged, dilemmas to be faced. Approaches to resolving these tensions need to be situated within the purposes of collecting disability data and acknowledging the different audiences. For schools the aim is to enable them to make changes to their policies, practices and procedures to ensure that disabled children are not discriminated against and are able to enjoy the same opportunities as their non-disabled peers. There is also a requirement for schools to be *proactive* in anticipating barriers that pupils could encounter together with monitoring the impact of their activities. These duties extend to local authorities and to government, audiences that require statistical data that lend themselves to wider comparisons and aggregation. While it would be simplistic to reduce this to differing needs for qualitative and quantitative information, for schools the information is highly contextualized with a requirement for more detail and specificity, for local authorities and government purposes the data will inevitably be reductive, a series of codes and categories within a database. In navigating our way through the literature we need to be cognizant of these differences, otherwise the full potential of the Act will be diminished. These differing purposes and audiences indicate the need for multiple approaches, one that is inherently inflexible that provides easily compared data and one that is flexible and adaptive to the local context. The following sections set out the core principles that were drawn from the conceptual literature that influenced the development of the tools.

Universality (and heterogeneity)

Adopting a universal approach to the collection of data makes no predictions about who is or isn't disabled. It's seen as part of the human condition, one that is not fixed and static but fluid and contextual. It avoids the false assumption that disability equates to a special educational need, or that only children with known impairments and health conditions are disabled. The literature has illustrated the uncertain relationships between impairment, functioning and disability. Reindal's discussion that impairment is a necessary but not sufficient requisite is useful here, although it assumes that the impairment or health condition is one that is recognized. The literature is powerful in relation to separating out health conditions from functioning and functioning from disability. As Barnes (2012) has highlighted, there are a number of impairments that don't impact on the capabilities of a person. Yet data on functionings are endemic to the way governments across the world collect disability information. Despite the rhetoric of the social model, they ask individuals to itemize the skills and abilities that are limited.

The review of the literature reveals the importance of adopting a model that reflects the heterogeneity of experiences, that recognizes the complex interaction between social, cultural and environmental factors but that also recognizes individual differences, including those arising from the child's health condition or impairment. The researchers adopted Shakespeare's interactional and relational understanding:

> The experience of a disabled person results from the relationship between factors intrinsic to the individual, and extrinsic factors arising from the wider context in which she finds herself. Among the intrinsic issues are factors such as the nature and severity of her impairment, her own attitudes to it, her personal qualities and abilities, and her personality. Among the contextual factors are: the attitudes and reactions of others, the extent to which the environment is enabling or disabling, and wider cultural, social and economic issues relevant to disability in that society.
>
> (Shakespeare 2006, pp. 55–56)

This enabled us to recognize and respond to internalized oppression as well as that externally provided. It has much in common with the position of Nordic disability writers and reflects the multiple contributing factors to the experience of a child with an impairment or health condition. We were aware however of the potential antagonism this would raise with people who adopt the 'strong' form of the social model, not least because the inclusion of personal aspects may be taken to dilute the importance of societal oppression.

Privileging subjective experience

The social model has changed the discourse on disability, promoted and empowered disabled people to take a full part in the decision-making of organizations. It foregrounds the experience of disabled people and actively resists attempts for others to speak on their behalf, however well-intentioned. The implications for schools are clear. Children's views need to be at the heart of the process of data collection, one which seeks to understand the barriers that they encounter. However, government statistical data are routinely provided by adults. Personal data are only collected from children over the age of 12 – and then not from all children. Parents therefore have a role to play in providing information that can inform government policy. Unlike special educational needs, disability is not confined to school settings. Children also encounter barriers to participation in settings other than school and these may be more significant in their lives than ones which centre around the school day. We need to be mindful when we collect data from children and their parents that they provide different perspectives and that one should not be privileged over the other.

Self-disclosure

Disability is self-disclosed, and not a result of a professional decision to label. It is not a neutral term and, as we have seen from other research, many children and parents will not identify with the term (Lewis *et al.* 2005; Watson 1999, 2002). For some there may be a trade-off, a weighing up of the advantages and the disadvantages of the term or, as Pullin (2008) states, 'the utility and the consequences' of the label. This is a central dilemma which all disability data collection methods face, as Bickenback *et al.* (1999), writing in the context of developing the WHO framework, state:

> Demands to end social inequality and discrimination require the researcher to identify those who have been disadvantaged, and that can only be done by drawing attention to their difference; yet if difference is ignored or downplayed to support the claim of equality, then the different needs of people may also be ignored.
>
> (p. 1177)

Norwich (2008), writing about provision for children with SEN, uses the phrase 'dilemmas of difference' to describe 'the problem of inequality can be aggravated either by treating members of a minority as the same as the majority or by treating them as different' (p. 8). Treating people differently can serve to emphasize differences and treating them the same can prove equally insensitive, the allocation of equal resources serves to maintain disadvantage yet is also argued to be a fair system. Thus he sets out the identification dilemma which we can view in relation to disability as: if children are identified as disabled then they may well be treated differently, devalued or even stigmatized but if they are not identified, then it is unlikely that they will receive additional resources or adaptations. The trade-off for some parents and children will reflect their confidence in how the information will be used and responded to.

Ethos

The context in which the data are collected is vitally important. The social model has increased recognition of the ways in which oppression operates. In current times of economic instability the allocation of finite and limited resources provides a magnifying glass to the values of society, 'the pursuit of profit over equality and social justice' (Barnes 2012, p. 23). Decisions about thresholds and cut-off points highlight those who are included and those who are excluded, and there will be vested interests in operation in schools. Marketization within education has led schools to make judgements between pupils on the basis of statistical normalcy. It is important that these tools are not seen as a way of weeding out expensive and/or deviant pupils.

The process of data collection therefore needs to be set within a positive school ethos. Schools have a vital role to play in contributing to the positive narratives around diversity and difference. Writers powerfully draw attention to the ways in which the responses of others, the language and discourse of difference contribute to the experience of an impairment. The portrayal and content of the data collection tools from children needs to support schools in understanding the diverse ways in which barriers operate and are experienced and promote the valuing of diversity and difference.

The literature has therefore led us to a two-pronged approach that involves collecting data from both parents and children – with both elements necessary to fulfil the duties set out in the legislation in a spirit that is compatible with the intentions of a human rights agenda, namely one that is transformative and empowering.

Chapter 3

Collecting disability data

Introduction

The previous chapter set out the conceptual underpinning for the development of tools to collect disability data. This resulted in a two-pronged approach. On the one hand there is a need for data that can be aggregated and used by schools, local authorities and other service providers, as well as the government to monitor the impact of policies, practices and procedures on disabled children and in order to do this identify children who meet the Equality Act definition. This information is required from parents in consultation with their children. The second approach is the development of tools that schools can use flexibly to find out directly about the experience of children and the barriers and supports to participation. This information enables schools to be both proactive and reactive in developing better places for learning. The focus of this chapter is the first approach. Previous attempts to collect disability data are reviewed, drawing out the evidence base that informed our decision-making for the technical development of a questionnaire for schools to use to collect data from *all* parents. At the same time we trialled and developed a number of activities that schools could adapt to use as tools to collect information from children as part of capturing the subjective experience rather than simply relying on the reports of others. The details of these activities are provided in Chapter 5.

It is perhaps surprising that despite the introduction of the Disability Discrimination Act in 1995 we do not have good systems for collecting disability data – particularly when it concerns information about children and young people. The Office for Disability Issues (2007) lists the challenges including a lack of clarity about definitions, poor coverage and understanding of disabled people's lives, a focus on impairments rather than barriers, and poor adaptation of adult items for use with children. Often in the past the data that were collected were tied to service provision, however this can limit data by service eligibility criteria and availability of resources. This approach also provides no record for those who don't receive a particular service, even though they may be eligible. Geographical areas that have the greatest level of resources will appear to have the greatest level of need. Service-driven data collection does have the advantage however that data collection is routinely collected, providing a year-on-year profile from which to readily identify changes. When Mooney *et al.* (2008) approached local authorities for their disability data, those who were able to provide an actual count (rather than an estimate) largely did so in relation to pupils with statements of special educational needs or those who received social care.

Some parts of the education system have been more proactive than others in recognizing the need to collect these data. The Learning and Skills Council funded a series of projects between 2003 and 2005 to promote the introduction of systems in colleges of further education and work-based learning centres. Their guidance in an aptly named publication, *Do You Have a Disability – Yes or No? Or Is There a Better Way of Asking?* (Rose 2006), demonstrates well the limitations of simply putting a question or two on an application form. Further education procedures were developed through consultation with disability groups. The projects were able to monitor the impact of changes made to their methods through comparison of disclosure levels year on year. These projects addressed issues of what questions are asked and how they are worded, the appearance and format of the form, the context of disclosure, the culture of the organization, all issues that I return to later in the chapter as it is clear that these can have a dramatic impact on people's willingness to indicate they have a disability.

Typically disability data are collected through structured methods. Most people will be familiar with the questions about disability that feature on employment and other forms. These often take the form 'do you have a disability?' or 'would you say you were disabled?' and require a yes or no answer (usually in the form of ticking a box). At best they enable the receiver of the form to monitor the organization's equal opportunities policy. More frequently however people will either respond automatically without consideration or conversely be uncertain about the implications of ticking the box, of what counts as a disability, or what degree of severity is implied. In practice therefore they do not serve well even as a screening device for follow-up. Mont (2007) provides evidence that these self-identification questions generate the lowest rates of disability, typically between 1 per cent and 3 per cent.

It is of course hardly surprising that a complex concept such as disability cannot be reduced to a single question, or even to a two-stage question, although this has been the basis on which data have been collected in the past as part of government-funded national household surveys. Before turning to look at technical aspects it is important to consider some broader factors that have shaped the development of data collection tools.

What can we learn from previous attempts?

The last 15 years have seen concerted attempts by worldwide organizations to develop ways of collecting data about disabled children. Robson and Evans (2003) for example compare the work of the World Bank, UNESCO, Unicef and the OECD in their early attempts to develop a classification framework. While these have been extensively reviewed and critiqued they have also largely been well funded and in consequence developed, trialled and tested over time. The result has been that we do know something about the strengths and limitations of different types of questioning and the extent to which this increases or reduces the disclosure of disability. We also know however that the majority of approaches have lacked a contextual element to their data collection. Indeed most reviews start from the premise that what is needed is a common tool that will provide some kind of culture-free measure that will enable cross-country comparisons. While on the one hand this may serve the needs of global organizations, what is needed here is one fit for our purposes.

Here in the UK Read et al. (2007) evaluated 30 different datasets focussing exclusively on the collection of data on children and young people under 18 years and note that none of these establishes the degree of restriction experienced by the child. Like other authors they reveal the large differences in prevalence rate depending on the questions, the age range of the sample, residency and geographical spread resulting in rates of between 5 per cent and 18 per cent. (We may view this as surprising but Gronvig (2008) in a review of Norweigan databases found differences of between 7 per cent and 32 per cent!) For example in the UK General Household Survey (2005/6) parents are asked if the child has 'any longstanding illness, disability or infirmity (ONS 2005). By long-standing I mean anything which has troubled [name] over a period of time or that is likely to affect him/her over a period of time?' They follow this up by asking 'what is the matter with [name]. Does this illness or disability limit [name] in any way?' This is followed by a third question asking whether they had to cut down or limit what they normally do in the previous two weeks. This questioning revealed that 18 per cent of children below the age of 18 who were living at home and in full-time education had a long-standing illness and 7 per cent of them were restricted in their activities by it. There are many limitations to the wording of these questions. Research by Langlois (2002) on the development of the Canadian survey tools revealed the negative effect of using the term long-standing. One might anticipate that the use of the term infirmity has a similar effect and it suggests that this is the adult question applied to a child. One might also question whether the previous two weeks captured those with cyclical experiences of disability or indeed those who were always restricted. Notably it does not refer to the degree of restriction.

The survey tool that comes closest to embracing the Equality Act definition is the Family Resources Survey, produced for the Department of Work and Pensions (ONS undated). In 2004/5 this included an interesting shift in the terminology used. It asked the same opening question as the General Household Survey using the terms illness, disability or infirmity. This was followed by asking 'Does this physical or mental illness or disability limit [child's name] in any way?' A third question was then asked: 'Does this/these health problems or disabilities mean that [child's name] has significant difficulties with any of these areas of his/her life. Exclude difficulties that you would expect for a child that age' and this was followed by a list of areas of functioning: mobility, lifting/carrying, manual dexterity, continence, communication (speech, hearing, eyesight), memory/ability to concentrate or understand, recognize if in physical danger, physical co-ordination, other problem or disability. This was followed up by a final question that asks about whether they take 'medication without which their health problems (when taken together) would significantly affect their life in the areas we have been discussing'. Based on these survey questions it is estimated that 6 per cent of children are disabled (DWP 2012a). Notably none of these questions other than referring generically to health conditions/problems, infirmities, physical or mental illness includes examples of the type of thing they might be referring to. They illustrate well however the challenge for survey providers in finding the right words and phrasing.

Box 3.1 Office for National Statistics (2011a) harmonized questions

Long-lasting health conditions and illnesses
Do you have any physical or mental health conditions or illnesses lasting or expected to last for 12 months or more?

1. Yes
2. No

Impairments
Do any of these conditions or illnesses affect you in any of the following areas?

1   Vision (for example blindness or partial sight)
2   Hearing (for example deafness or partial hearing)
3   Mobility (for example walking short distances or climbing stairs)
4   Dexterity (for example lifting and carrying objects, using a keyboard)
5   Learning or understanding or concentrating
6   Memory
7   Mental health
8   Stamina or breathing or fatigue
9   Socially or behaviourally (for example associated with autism, attention deficit disorder or Asperger's syndrome)
10 Other (please specify)

Activity restriction
Does your condition or illness/do any of your conditions or illnesses reduce your ability to carry-out day-to-day activities?

1   Yes, a lot
2   Yes, a little
3   Not at all

Most recently the Office of National Statistics has attempted to harmonize the way in which disability data are collected and specifically address the way in which household survey data have mixed 'the concepts of illness, disability and infirmity'. As a result there are now three key questions that should be included and these are shown in Box 3.1. The reader will quickly note that this also is not a perfect measure, particularly so where children are concerned. Questions on impairment and activity limitation serve to exclude three groups that are included by the Equality Act 2010:

1   those with one of the progressive conditions specified in the act (e.g. HIV/ AIDS, cancer or multiple sclerosis) whether or not the condition has a substantial adverse effect carrying out day-to-day activities;
2   those who would be restricted without medication or treatment;
3   those that have been restricted in the past but are no longer restricted.

Questions on impairment also do not include awareness of danger or risk that are fundamental to many of the activity limitations experienced by families. The Office was perhaps compromised by the need to capture data for reporting back to the European Union's Statistics on Income and Living Conditions (EU-SILC), illustrating the challenges of collecting data for more than one purpose.

The review by Read and colleagues (2009) also concluded that survey 'questions invariably assume that individual impairments or conditions are the primary determinant of social and personal restriction' and none of the datasets had 'refined ways of establishing the extent of the limitation experienced by the child' (p. 138).

Our task was therefore to remedy these deficits through ensuring a broader coverage of impact by looking at activity and participation, by having a measure of impact and a space for parents to indicate the barriers and supports for their child.

Starting points in the collection of disability data

The Advisory Committee on Australian and International Disability Data (2005) has provided useful practical guidelines for those authorities who are developing survey devices of this kind. The following questions provide a number of key decisions for organizations to make, some of which I draw on here.

1   What do you want to use the information for?
2   What specifically do you need to know from the data?
3   How often are the data to be collected?
4   Who will use the data?
5   How are the data to be collated and analyzed?

6   About whom exactly will you collect data? (Including age, is it everyone, or targeted groups)

7   How will you tell people about the purposes and uses of the collection, how will you give people confidence about access to information/storage of this information?

8   What will trigger the collection of the data (time, event, etc.)?

9   What medium will be used to collect data, ask questions?

10   Who will provide the answers?

11   What resources are needed to collect the data – time, people etc.?

12   How will the tools be piloted?

Establishing the purpose

It's important to be clear about the purpose of collecting the data and what they are to be used for. One of the limitations of the surveys we have reviewed above is the multi-purpose nature of the data collection designed to inform government policy and to monitor changes that relate to government targets. Where one of the purposes is comparison over time, key questions will be kept largely static and not reflect changes in understanding. The Equality Act 2010 sets out the prime purpose that disabled people should not be treated unfairly (less favourably than other people). For schools, therefore, the purpose of the data collection is knowing how many disabled pupils there are, and who they are, so that they can:

- monitor their educational achievements over time;
- monitor their opportunities and access to participation in all aspects of school life; e.g. position of responsibility in school; satisfaction and enjoyment across a range of school activities; aspirations and ambitions for the future; access to work placements; take up of careers advice;
- identify the supports they find helpful and the barriers they encounter.

An additional purpose for local authorities may be to monitor their access to services and identify unmet service needs. When we consulted with local authorities as part of our developmental work (Porter *et al.* 2008), the only additional information they wanted to include was a specific question about autistic spectrum disorder as this was a particular area of service where they needed additional information.

Knowing what data are needed

Having clarified the purpose of the data collection and what the information is to be used for, after the next step in decision-making is to be clear about the actual data that are required. Collecting data for data's sake is time-consuming (and costly), complex to store and analyze and de-motivating for all participants.

If we look again at the definition put forward in the Equality Act 2010 we will see that it includes a number of distinct elements:

- the presence of an impairment or health condition;
- that has gone on a year or more, or is likely to;
- has an impact on everyday activities;
- that is substantial;
- or would have an impact but for the use of medication or aids.

Questions about health conditions

Given the Equality Act definition there needs to be some question relating to establishing that the child has a health condition that is long-standing, that is has gone on for 12 months or more or is likely to (although there is an interesting issue of the extent that this information contributes to schools' understandings of the challenges faced by pupils). Including a list does enable parents to understand the range of health conditions that could be covered, that for example it includes children with mental health difficulties, a group that is often overlooked in child survey devices. Interestingly one of the further education project groups asked for the conditions to be listed in alphabetical order. This enables conditions to be easily found but also avoids the risk by implication that some conditions are more disabling than others. The list is unlikely to be exhaustive or inclusive and therefore if the data are important they will need to also be asked whether they have seen a professional and what the diagnosis was. Hutchison and Gordon (2005) counsel that only just over half of disabled children have a medical diagnosis. This is especially true for children with an intellectual impairment where terms such as global developmental delay, developmental disability or learning difficulty are given as broad descriptors rather than causal accounts. Parents are also likely to vary in the extent to which they recall the exact diagnosis, especially when they have been given different diagnoses at different times.

We added an additional question as research indicated that one of the invisible groups of children are those who return to school having had a serious accident or trauma. Although in general safety figures are reducing, some 16,500 children aged 5–15 were involved in road accidents in 2011 (Department of Transport 2012). Typically the return to school is seen as the pupil having recovered yet the experience of those who work with children who have been brain injured through car accidents and the like is that they continue to experience a range of difficulties that impact on their learning and participation in school activities (Rees 2007). Equally children that have experienced an emotional trauma that has left them with some mental health difficulties may not be understood by their parents to have a health condition.

As a result of these considerations the following questions were asked (see Figure 3.1).

Has your child had an accident or psychological trauma (e.g. loss of someone close) in the last 5 years that has seriously limited their activities either at home or school?

☐ Yes   ☐ No

If yes please describe:	If more than one incident please describe:
Month / Year it happened: ..../..........	Month / Year it happened: ..../..........

Does your child have a physical or mental health condition, impairment or difficulty such as: anxiety or depression, arthritis, asthma, autism, cancer, diabetes, epilepsy, hearing or visual impairment, HIV, Chronic Fatigue Syndrome (ME), mental health difficulty, mobility problems, learning difficulty, physical difficulties or a severe disfigurement?

☐ Yes   ☐ No   ☐ Unsure

If you answered yes:

Has the physical or mental health condition, impairment or difficulty gone on for a year or more (or is it likely to)?

☐ Yes   ☐ No   ☐ Unsure

Has your child seen a professional (e.g. paediatrician, psychologist) because of the physical or mental health condition, impairment or difficulty?

☐ Yes   ☐ No   ☐ Unsure

Figure 3.1 Questions about health conditions.

Questions about impact

As we have seen survey devices typically ask about functioning or capacity. One of the simplest screening devices, and one recommended for international use with children, was 'The Ten Questions', described by Robson and Evans (2003) as the 'best game in town' (p. 38). It was incorporated by Unicef in its Multiple Indicator Cluster Survey (MICS) and is still favoured by developing countries as a screening device that can be used with little training to identify children having difficulty in functioning in at least one domain (Unicef 2012). Of course functional difficulties lie along a continuum and many children catch up with time. They also rely on the respondent having experience or knowledge of other children to respond to such items as: 'Compared with other children, does or did [name] have any serious delay in sitting, standing or walking?', 'Does [name] learn to do things like other children his/her age?'. Westbrook *et al.* (1998) suggest that *only* using this type of criteria under-identifies disabled children although arguably it may also lead to false positives as children's acquisition of these skills might be delayed due to limited opportunities or a challenging environment. Simply asking whether the child has difficulty seeing or hearing is not a good identifier of children with visual or hearing problems.

Questions about activities and participation

Typically these two aspects are covered together yet arguably they involve two different things. Official guidance (ODI 2010) states:

> In general, day-to-day activities are things people do on a regular or daily basis, and examples include shopping, reading and writing, having a conversation or using the telephone, watching television, getting washed and dressed, preparing and eating food, carrying out household tasks, walking and travelling by various forms of transport, and taking part in social activities.
>
> (p. 31)

The disability module of the Health Survey for England in 2001 asked all those over the age of ten years old: 'what is the furthest you can walk on your own without discomfort?'. Items of this type prompt an important debate about the distinction between capacity and performance, i.e. what they could do compared with what they actually do. The former typically exceeds the latter in real life. The guidance also makes a distinction between capacity and how that impacts on activities. So for example a person with limited mobility may experience difficulty getting around unaided or using a normal means of transport; and this incapacity may impact on activities that involve leaving home with or without assistance; walking a short distance; climbing stairs; travelling in a car or completing a journey on public transport; sitting, standing, bending or reaching; or getting around in an unfamiliar place.

The parallel child-based questions are presented by the DfES (DfES/DRC 2006) under the heading 'Is Tom Disabled?'.

Does Tom have a difficulty with any of the following 'normal day-to-day activities'?

Mobility: getting to/from school, moving about the school and/or going on school visits?

Manual dexterity: holding a pen, pencil or book, using tools in design and technology, playing a musical instrument, throwing and catching a ball?

Physical co-ordination: washing or dressing, taking part in games and physical education?

Ability to lift, carry or otherwise move everyday objects: carrying a full school bag or other fairly heavy items?

Continence: going to the toilet or controlling the need to go to the toilet?

Speech: communicating with others or understanding what others are saying; how they express themselves orally or in writing?

Hearing: hearing what people say in person or on a video, DVD, radio or tape recording?

Eyesight: ability to see clearly (with spectacles/contact lenses where necessary), including any visual presentations in the classroom?

Memory or ability to concentrate, learn or understand: work in school including reading, writing, number work or understanding information?

Perception of the risk of physical danger: inability to recognize danger, e.g. when jumping from a height, touching hot objects or crossing roads?

Given that these capacity questions are used across a range of survey devices, we included these questions in our survey, although with some concern that parents of children with profound and multiple learning difficulties might find this kind of checklist rather a negative précis of their child's capacities.

The important distinction between capacity and performance makes it important to ask about what the child usually does. If the purpose of the question is to assess participation in the community then the measure should be sensitive to the circumstances and environment of that person (Young *et al.* 1996). Arguably these types of items are still routed in functional limitations rather than active participation and in our survey we therefore also elected to ask broader general questions about participation in school, home and community activities. Taking part can be as much about social relationships as about being able to perform a particular activity. At the heart lies the experience of feeling engaged and included. A broad question also allows the respondent to bring their own expectations and values to bear on the answer, to reflect lifestyle choices, the rituals and routines that are part and parcel of daily family life.

An additional element of impact was to ask whether the difficulties or health condition led to the child being absent from school. This resulted in the following three questions being asked (see Figure 3.2).

Does your child have any difficulty that affects his or her:

	Yes	Sometimes	No	Don't know
Classroom learning?				
Interaction with his or her classmates / peers?				
Joining in other school activities e.g. lunchtimes, breaks, social and leisure activities in school?				

Does your child have any difficulty that affects his or her:

	Yes	Sometimes	No
Daily activities such as eating, dressing, communicating, moving around, going to the toilet?			
Taking a full part in activities at home?			
Taking part in activities outside the home?			

Does your child have a difficulty which means that they are sometimes absent from school?

☐ Yes   ☐ No

Figure 3.2 Questions about participation.

Questions about degree of impact

In the first version of the questionnaire we trialled asking parents about impact using a scale of severity – mild, moderate, severe or profound impact – not dissimilar to that used by the ICF-CY. It is worth looking at what difference it makes (see Table 3.1).

In total 206 parents said their child had a moderate or greater impact on daily life. However a further 184 reported their children experienced an impact occasionally, including a small group of pupils in special schools. Depending therefore on where the cut-off point is placed can add almost 50 per cent to the sample. It also raised the incidence of disability in this first study from 7 per cent to 13 per cent.

On reflection the use of these terms, despite the descriptors that were used alongside them, could have been confusing to parents of children with SEN who were familiar with those descriptors being used together with learning difficulty. We therefore removed those terms and linked measures of impact

Table 3.1 Pilot impact measures

Overall how would you describe the impact of the difficulty (or difficulties)?	Primary	Secondary	Special	Total
Mild – *occasionally* interferes with everyday activities and only in a *minor* way	98	68	18	184
Moderate – *intermittent* but *regular* limitation of daily activities	41	26	43	110
Severe – *frequent and significant* impact on daily activities	18	13	38	69
Profound – unable to take part in a number of daily activities	1	1	25	27
Total	158	108	124	390

Overall, how does the physical or mental health condition, impairment or difficulty (when taken together) affect your child in their daily life? (Please tick one only)

a) No difficulty. My child can take a full part in home, community and school activities	
b) Occasionally it interferes with everyday activities but only in a *minor* way – there is an impact but it is trivial or small	
c) There are particular times and situations when activities are regularly stopped or limited because of the difficulty	
d) It frequently affects a number of daily activities	
e) The impact is felt on almost all activities every day	

Figure 3.3 Questions about degree of impact.

more directly to the different ways in which these might be experienced, using the following response options as indicative of the degree of impact (see Figure 3.3).

Questions about barriers and supports

There are relatively few published examples of closed questions in relation to what facilitates and what hinders a child from taking part in activities in the home, school or community. The Life Opportunities Survey includes the following items:

> There are many reasons why people can't take part in activities as much as they would like to.

Is <name of child> limited in the following areas of life for any reason …
  (1) Education?
  (2) Leisure or play?
  (3) Transport?
  (4) Personal relationships?
  (5) None of these

What limits him/her in these areas?
  (1) Financial reasons
  (2) Too busy/not enough time
  (3) A health condition, illness or impairment
  (4) A disability
  (5) Poor services
  (6) Lack of help or assistance
  (7) Lack of special aids or equipment
  (8) Badly designed buildings
  (9) Attitudes of others
  (10) Lack of information

The inclusion of 'a disability' as a limit to participation is a confusing distractor in this question. The ICF WHO items require an indication of the degree of severity (none, mild, moderate, severe, extreme/cannot do) in relation to:

> How much of a problem did you have because of barriers or hindrances in the world around you?
> How much of a problem did you have living with dignity because of the attitudes and actions of others?

We adopted an open question, anticipating that schools would like more detailed information that would help them to understand what sort of response would be helpful. However even an open question requires some prompts to encourage the participant to consider the variety of ways in which the child is and could be supported.

Language and phrasing

It will have become clear by now that there are a myriad of possible questions that could be asked and the language that is used has important effects on the way people respond to a survey device. Disability is not a neutral term. ORB (2004 cited by the DRC 2005) surveyed 1,000 disabled people and found that none of them agreed with the description 'I am disabled' and were much more likely to feel they were better described by 'I have a health condition' or similar. Indeed in some cultures disability is viewed as a punishment for sins in an earlier life. A series of studies by Lewis and colleagues for the Disability

Rights Commission suggested that many parents preferred the term difficulty to disability. Children's development and learning fluctuate and there may be uncertainty about their trajectory and this may well contribute to a reluctance to assign a descriptor to their child that seems overly predictive of the longer term (Lewis *et al.* 2005). Given these issues it was decided to use the term difficulty alongside that of impairment and health condition.

Questionnaires require an explanatory introduction to ensure that the recipient knows why they are being asked the questions as well as any instructions for completion. It is also a place to ensure that issues of confidentiality are addressed and people are told what will happen to the data and how they will be used. While the first versions of the questionnaire were headed 'Promoting Disability Equality', we realized that inadvertently we had suggested that only parents who considered their child disabled should complete it. Given a lack of understanding about disability and the negative connotations of the term this led to parents returning the questionnaire uncompleted. The overriding purpose of the questionnaire was to 'make schools better places for learning' and this therefore became the strapline that we used. We also ensured that there was a fast-track through the questionnaire and that our initial questions served to ensure that all parents were encouraged to consider if their child experienced any significant difficulties participating and were offered the opportunity to talk to a member of staff.

The items on a questionnaire, phrasing of questions, how it is introduced and presented all give important messages that parents will interpret in the light of how they understand the ethos of the school. Parents will complete the questionnaire on the understanding that something will happen as a result. In consequence people's expectations need to be managed. In the current study this was done through a covering letter that explained about the concept of reasonable adjustments.

Piloting the questionnaire

The final questionnaire was a result of extensive development and piloting work. We tested out three alternatives with schools, using a different ordering and wording of questions, gaining qualitative feedback from parents and schools in order to gauge:

* How well the structured tools identified individuals with disability.
* Whether parents were willing and easily able to complete them.
* How well the information met stakeholder needs.

The result was to amalgamate two of the questionnaires and to avoid beginning the questionnaire with a disability question. Instead the starting point was to encourage the respondent to reflect on the experiences of their child. We also changed the strapline, made sure that there was a response option for all parents

– often adding a 'not sure' or 'don't know' category. This refined questionnaire was then tested with 74 schools across ten local authorities. Further government funding enabled us to test it further with an additional 49 schools and to look specifically at how schools analyzed and used the information following guidance provided by the research team. The final version can be found in the appendix.

Such extensive development work, while unusual on the one hand, is characteristic of developing appropriate tools to identify children with disability. While we were not as ambitious as world organizations such as Unicef or the World Health Organization in developing a tool for global use, development work and extensive testing has proved an essential part of creating a tool fit for a national census. The next section of this chapter provides a brief analysis of some of the data in order to draw attention both to the importance of using multiple items but also to surface the contextual and cultural nature of the data.

Findings

Presented below are the findings from the second phase of the project with the sample comprised of 49 schools, from 11 local authorities across the country, representing urban, rural and inner-city provision. The schools were nominated by their local authorities, usually (but not always) with their prior consent. Of the 49 schools, 25 (51 per cent) were primary schools, 15 (31 per cent) secondary and nine (18 per cent) special schools. The latter included one school for pupils with behaviour, emotional and social difficulties (BESD), two schools that were designated for pupils with moderate learning difficulties (MLD) and six that were designated for those with severe learning difficulties (SLD). In addition the sample included a range of resourced mainstream provision, including one primary school with a unit for children with a hearing impairment, another with provision for children with ASD, and a third for severe language and communication difficulties and three secondary schools with additional special provision, one with a unit for pupils with profound and multiple learning difficulties (PMLD), one resource provision for pupils with specific learning difficulties (SpLD) and a third with integrated MLD and SLD provision.

The 49 schools sent out 6,208 parental questionnaires, 2,382 (38 per cent) primary, 3,426 (55 per cent) secondary and 400 (6 per cent) special. The overall return rate was 41 per cent, with 2,537 questionnaires returned to schools, 72

Table 3.2 Return rates by school level

School level	Average return rates	Minimum return rate	Maximum return rate
Primary	51%	27%	71%
Secondary	35%	5%	83%
Special	49%	31%	75%

of them online. The average masks considerable differences between schools and secondary schools provided both the highest (83 per cent) and lowest (5 per cent) response rate.

Returns from mainstream education were evenly split with an overall 50:50 ratio. Boys were over-represented in the returns from special schools, with a ratio of 71 per cent boys to 29 per cent girls, reflecting the national census data for special schools (DCSF 2007).

Schools chose which year groups to send the questionnaires to and, as a result, three primary schools and three special schools opted to send the questionnaire to the whole school and a further six primary schools chose two year groups. Others chose a single year group. The result is that the age range of the sample peaked for ages 11–12 as shown in Figure 3.4.

The starting point for legislation is the presence of an impairment or health condition so this is the starting place for the analysis. Table 3.3 reveals the uncertainty to which parents respond to this question with 55 (2 per cent) of parents either leaving the question blank or indicating they were unsure.

The majority of the respondents, 1,899 (75 per cent), answered no to this question but 583 (23 per cent) answered yes. This number was further reduced in the subsequent question which asked whether it had gone on a year or more, with 534 (21 per cent) indicating that it fulfilled the criteria of long-standing. Again there were a small number of parents (38) indicating they were not sure.

These two questions were followed by questions relating to whether the child had been seen by a professional and received a diagnosis. These subsequent questions serve to further refine the number of children who *might* be disabled. The data reveal that there is some ambiguity around asking parents if they

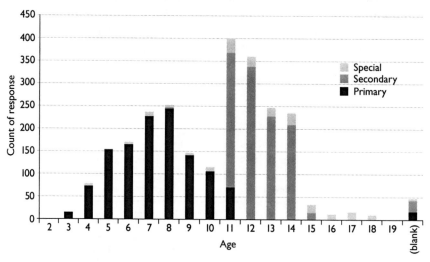

Figure 3.4 Distribution of pupil age by phase.

Table 3.3 Number of children with a health condition, impairment or difficulty

Q4i Does your child have a physical or mental health condition, impairment or difficulty?	Primary	Secondary	Special	Grand total
No	992	906	1	1,899
Unsure	23	10	2	35
Yes	197	193	193	583
(blank)	10	10		20
Grand total	1,222	1,119	196	2,537

Table 3.4 Number of children with a long-standing health condition who have seen a professional and been given a diagnosis

	Primary	Secondary	Special	Totals
Parents whose child had a health condition that had gone on for a year or more	173	179	182	534
And who indicated they had seen a professional	165	161	176	502
And been given a diagnosis	159	169	165	493

have seen a professional, all children in special schools for example would have seen a professional at some stage prior to admission even if they had not yet formally received a statement of special educational need. Although the question included examples of professionals they might have seen, parents can still be unclear about which professionals qualify. They may also have forgotten who they saw. This may also explain why more parents of secondary school pupils were able to provide a diagnosis than indicate they had seen a professional.

Issues of diagnosis are by no means straightforward as the following quotes illustrate:

In the past Heather was tested for dyslexia, absence epilepsy and ADD. No condition identified although recommendations were made.

Very tired all the time, no diagnosis found at the moment!

Very complex issues – delayed development language difficulties – emotional difficulties …

At the moment – specific learning difficulties & developmental coordination disorder, still waiting for more information from Paediatrician, when she has spoken further with school.

These comments are similar to those gathered as part of the first study and illustrate the incompleteness of the diagnosis for many children, the time taken, and that it can be a very frustrating experience for parents.

> we have seen the world and his grandma. Non specific. within autistic spectrum. microcephally epilepsy. learning difficulty.

> has varied. Speech and Language impairment, social communication difficulties and Asperger syndrome have all been mentioned but no definitive label attributed.

This last quote also demonstrates that diagnosis can mean several different things; the identification of a particular medical condition, the presence of particular recognized difficulties, or of the symptoms that a child experiences. In consequence, when asked about the diagnosis, parents provide differing types and levels of information. The lack of certainty around diagnosis may go some way to explaining why some parents may be uncertain about whether their child has a mental or physical health condition or impairment.

Children who had experienced an accident or trauma

The questionnaire also asked parents if the child had experienced a significant accident or trauma. In total parents of 105 children indicated on the form that this had been the case. However many of these were included in the group above, but five children experienced continued difficulties, three had mental health disorders resulting from an incident and two had mobility difficulties as a result of an accident. Data from these five are therefore added to our larger sample. The presence of a trauma, health condition or impairment is not synonymous with being disabled. For this we need to consider these children in relation first to the overall impact of the difficulties.

Impact on daily life

A significant and pivotal aspect of the Equality Act criteria is that the impairment or condition has a substantial (i.e. not trivial) impact on daily life. Children whose parents responded that the child experienced no difficulty or that they only experienced an occasional impact and then it was minor or trivial were removed from this group, effectively halving the number who met the disability criteria. Data on the experience of impact by the remainder are shown in Table 3.5. In some cases the impact was felt on almost all activities. This included 45 per cent of the pupils in special schools, 13 per cent in secondary schools and 27 per cent in primary schools. In mainstream settings, the impact was more likely to occur at particular times and situations, although notably the distribution across categories of impact was more evenly spread in the primary schools.

Table 3.5 Impact level by school

Q6 *Overall how does this affect your child in their daily life?*	Primary N=59	Secondary N=54	Special N=157	Grand total N=270
There are particular times and situations when activities are regularly stopped or limited because of the difficulty	23 (39%)	33 (61%)	48 (31%)	104 (39%)
It frequently affects a number of daily activities	20 (34%)	14 (26%)	38 (24%)	72 (27%)
The impact is felt on almost all activities every day	16 (27%)	7 (13%)	71 (45%)	94 (35%)

In total therefore 270 children were identified who met the legal disability criteria, 59 in primary schools, 54 in secondary and 157 in special schools, a prevalence rate for the returned sample of 5 per cent in both primary and secondary schools and 80 per cent in special schools, or, taken together, 11 per cent of the total sample. This is slightly higher than the 7 per cent reported by the government (Cabinet Office 2005). The gender divide in primary schools was more uneven (72 per cent boys and 38 per cent girls) than secondary schools (46 per cent boys and 54 per cent girls). It is unclear why prevalence rates for boys are higher in primary schools, although it could reflect the inclusion of a primary school with an autistic class in our sample. National figures for disability are generally only slightly higher for mild disability in boys although substantially higher for severe disability (ONS 2004).

Impact and participation

If we look at the data on participation (Table 3.6) we can see where the impact is most likely to be experienced. Looking across our sample there were differences both in the overall percentage of children experiencing difficulties in different areas of life and in the proportion of these for whom the difficulty occurred only sometimes. For both primary and secondary school children the proportion of children experiencing difficulties just sometimes was smaller than those who answered yes. The same was true for secondary school pupils except with respect to activities inside and outside the home. Overall rates were higher for special school pupils than mainstream. With these distinctions in mind one of the greatest areas of difficulty lay with participation in school. Looking across the three groups, 86 per cent of the children experienced difficulties participating in classroom learning (of these 16 per cent only sometimes) and 87 per cent in activities outside the home (of these 28 per cent only sometimes). Overall 79 per cent experienced difficulty interacting with peers (21 per cent only sometimes). Other school activities are difficult for 76 per cent of children (25 per cent only sometimes). Secondary school children in general were less likely to experience difficulty across every setting compared with primary or special

Table 3.6 Parents' ratings of children's experiences of participation

Experiences difficulty participating in:		Primary N=59	Secondary N=54	Special N=157	Total number of children N=270
Classroom learning	Yes	42 (71%)	19 (35%)	129 (82%)	190 (70%)
	Sometimes	9 (15%)	14 (26%)	21 (13%)	44 (16%)
Interactions with other pupils	Yes	33 (56%)	14 (26%)	110 (70%)	157 (58%)
	Sometimes	13 (22%)	13 (24%)	32 (20%)	58 (21%)
Other school activities (e.g. lunchtimes, breaks, social and leisure activities in school	Yes	33 (56%)	17 (31%)	89 (57%)	139 (51%)
	Sometimes	10 (17%)	12 (22%)	45 (29%)	67 (25%)
Daily activities (such as eating, dressing, communicating, moving around, going to the toilet)	Yes	34 (58%)	14 (26%)	108 (69%)	156 (58%)
	Sometimes	13 (22%)	12 (22%)	41 (26%)	66 (24%)
Activities at home	Yes	27 (46%)	10 (19%)	98 (62%)	135 (50%)
	Sometimes	18 (31%)	19 (35%)	46 (29%)	83 (31%)
Activities outside the home	Yes	30 (51%)	12 (22%)	116 (74%)	158 (59%)
	Sometimes	19 (32%)	24 (44%)	32 (20%)	75 (28%)

school children, and parents were as likely to rate this as sometimes occurring as making a general yes statement. Given that the prevalence rate in primary and secondary schools in our data are the same it would appear that difficulties with participation are reduced with age, or at least in the view of parents.

Parents' description of need

Given this profile of participation it is perhaps unsurprising that the largest category of need (Table 3.7) was in the area of learning (77 per cent of children) followed in order of size by communication (71 per cent) and behaviour (61 per cent), and these three areas of need were the dominant ones across all three phases of education. Notably however, as shown in Table 3.7, mental health difficulties and difficulties with eating and drinking are also prevalent areas of need amongst the identified pupils in secondary provision. Fifty-seven children in mainstream settings had no learning difficulty/special educational need. This constitutes some 50 per cent of the mainstream sample.

Many children had multiple areas of need with eight children having a total of 11 identified areas of need. As might be expected pupils in special schools were more likely to have multiple needs and pupils in mainstream having a markedly higher proportion with a single area of need identified.

Table 3.7 Areas of need by phase of school

Q7 How is your child affected … please tick any that apply.	Primary N=59	Secondary N=54	Special N=157	Grand total N=270
a) Mobility: getting around in or outside the home	23 (39%)	14 (26%)	74 (47%)	111 (41%)
b) Hand function: holding and touching	21 (36%)	4 (7%)	49 (31%)	74 (27%)
c) Personal care: has difficulty washing, going to the toilet, dressing	28 (47%)	7 (13%)	105 (67%)	140 (52%)
d) Eating and drinking: has difficulty eating or drinking by themselves or sickness or lack of appetite	17 (29%)	12 (22%)	54 (34%)	83 (31%)
e) Incontinence: has difficulty controlling the passage of urine and/or faeces	19 (32%)	5 (9%)	59 (38%)	83 (31%)
f) Communication: speaking and/or understanding others	37 (63%)	15 (28%)	139 (89%)	191 (71%)
g) Learning: has special educational needs	36 (61%)	19 (35%)	153 (97%)	208 (77%)
h) Hearing	12 (20%)	3 (6%)	16 (10%)	31 (11%)
i) Vision	7 (12%)	1 (2%)	40 (25%)	48 (18%)
j) Behaviour: has a condition that leads to the child being hyperactive or having a short attention span or getting frustrated or behaving in a socially unacceptable manner	37 (63%)	16 (30%)	113 (72%)	166 (61%)
k) Consciousness: has fits or seizures	3 (5%)	1 (2%)	30 (19%)	34 (13%)
l) Diagnosed with Autism, Asperger Syndrome or Autistic Spectrum Disorder (ASD)	18 (31%)	7 (13%)	80 (51%)	105 (39%)
m) Palliative care needs	1 (2%)	1 (2%)	4 (3%)	6 (2%)
n) Mental health needs e.g. depression, anxiety	8 (14%)	13 (24%)	34 (22%)	55 (20%)
o) Other	3 (5%)	7 (13%)	0	10 (4%)
No needs	1 (2%)	5 (9%)	0	6 (2%)

Relationship between impact and need

Need (or functioning) has been used in the past as synonymous with impact and therefore indicative of disability (Bryson *et al.* 2008; DES/DRC 2006). It was clear from our data that this relationship was rather more complex. Level of need was not a true or exact indicator of impact and not all of the children with identified areas of need met the legal criteria for disability as parents report no substantial impact. Eleven pupils in our group of children with a long-standing health condition or impairment had five or more areas of need, but reported no impact. Three of them were placed in primary schools but the majority were in special schools. Their parents had either reported that the impact was trivial or small (eight instances) or that there was no difficulty (two) or left the question blank (one). This led us to further interrogate the data to look at the relationship between need, impact and diagnosis.

One positive inference is that the school and other agencies have provided optimum levels of support as we can see from the following quotes:

> My son leads a normal life within school and home by using walker, stader, bench, wedge, talk machine, leckey chair and a disabled bike. All my son's hospital team, staff at school, myself and family do everything to make him happy.
>
>> (Mother of a six-year-old boy who attends a special school with eight areas of need (mobility, hand function, personal care, eating, incontinence, communication, fits and LD) which only occasionally impacted on daily life)

> He has a brilliant support team at his school. This enables him to participate in all subjects. We continue to work at home via interaction from school.
>
>> (Mother of a 16-year-old boy who attends [same special school] with nine areas of need (vision, hearing, mobility, hand function, personal care, eating, incontinence, communication, and LD) and his parent indicating 'a) No difficulty. Medication/aids/equipment allow my child to take a full part in home, community and school activities')

Both parents have children in special schools, and given their profile of needs one might anticipate they would experience difficulties participating in some settings. Age does not appear of be a factor here which contradicts an assumption that younger children are easier to accommodate in family life.

At the other end of continuum is the following example of a nine-year-old boy in primary school whose mother reports no other needs except learning difficulty, no impairment or health condition but the impact is felt on almost all activities every day.

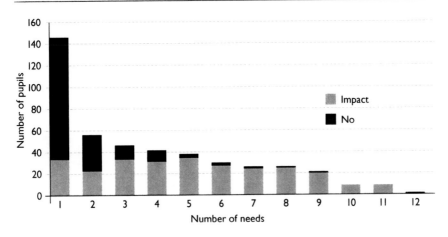

Figure 3.5 Pupils with one or more areas of need and their experience of impact (N=450).

School supportive, extra help before school with literacy/computers
Really needs 1:1 in the classroom
Already been addressed.

The comment suggests that the school is making reasonable adjustments, and yet the impact is felt on participation. Another example is of a 14–year-old girl in a secondary school with learning difficulties and anxiety whose parent reports that the impact is felt on almost all activities every day.

If we look at the data on need and impact, there were 450 children whose parents indicated that they had one or more areas of need. Of these 182 experienced no impact. Although we see that in general more children experience impact with greater levels of need, there are individuals for whom this is not true.

Diagnosis, need and impact

To investigate this further we looked at children with a common diagnosis, one which was not based around clusters of symptoms for which impact would already be related in some way. We therefore looked at the children with Down syndrome (DS). There were 17 in this phase of the project, 12 of whom met the criteria for disability as parents reported a substantial impact. Two of these children were in mainstream primary schools, one whose parent had identified six areas of need and one with eight. The five children whose parents don't report an impact have between two and seven areas of need.

The quotes from parents below further illustrate that there is a complex relationship between need and impact, and in the experience of support.

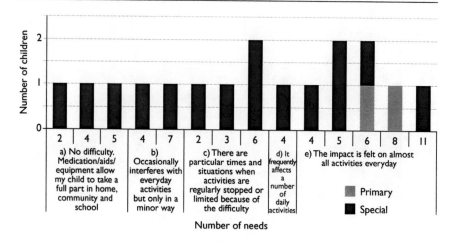

Figure 3.6 Needs and impact for children with Down syndrome (N=17).

The help from early years giving support so my daughter can attend kids club is really good. Support at school has been brilliant.

> (Ten-year-old girl in primary school with six areas of need and whose parent indicates that 'e) The impact is felt on almost all activities every day' is equally positive about the school)

It is particularly helpful that the high level of support is in place at school which enables Matt to fully participate in all daily activities at school.

> (16-year-old boy with DS attending a special school. Four areas of need. Mother reports no difficulty in participating)

Some conclusions for the methods of data collection

At the start of this chapter the inadequacy of simply asking people if they were disabled was discussed. The data from this study reveal some of the uncertainties in parents' responses to being asked the standard question about the presence of an impairment or health condition and the diagnoses. Not all conditions are clear-cut, the diagnosis resting on clusters of symptoms that can leave professionals uncertain. Parents may additionally be unsure as their child is growing and developing which 'symptoms' are significant, whether they are enduring or simply a phase that the child will pass through. Having examined the data therefore it is now also apparent that establishing the presence of a health condition or impairment is also clearly inadequate. The introduction of an impact 'measure' reveals the much smaller number of children who are disabled. In the previous survey we set the impact measure lower and as a result included more children. The establishment of a cut-off point is a political issue as it relates to the allocation of resources. The addition of participation questions indicated what an important issue this was for schools as well as those services that support children and young people at home and in the community.

It should also be noted that half of the mainstream sample were recorded as not having a learning difficulty. This is significant given the use of proxy SEN measures to indicate levels of disability, as it suggests that this ignores children who are performing at the expected level, including those who have the potential to achieve at higher levels given the appropriate support from school.

The data also revealed that need was an imperfect measure of impact. There are important contextual and cultural factors at work here. How families respond to areas of need will be different. Family life and expectations vary. This finding is consistent with studies examining quality of life and impairment. Pan-European studies of children with cerebral palsy have found that severity of impairment is not a significant variable in scores on quality of life measures – providing that it is not accompanied by pain (Dickinson *et al.* 2007; White-Koning *et al.* 2005). As quality of life scores are designed to reflect 'an individual's position in life in the context of the culture and value systems in which they live' (WHO 1995) it suggests that likewise our findings might be rooted in the ways in which the culture and values of families operate. Research with disabled adults posit that wellbeing is a function of developing a resilient attitude. Albrecht and Devlieger (1999) argue that using data from their qualitative interviews with disabled adults that 'having a can do approach to life; finding a purpose, meaning and harmony in life; having a spiritual foundation and outlook; constructing and living in a reciprocal social world' (p.984) can contribute to a sense of wellbeing. The data are a reminder of differences in the way that an impairment is experienced, and the importance of schools recognizing this.

The next chapter examines the qualitative data from parents on what their child finds supportive or enabling.

Chapter 4

What data tell us about the support parents value

A key purpose of the disability data collection tools is to understand how schools can support their disabled children and remove barriers to participation. Central to the definition of disability is the experience of a health condition or impairment and its impact on participation in daily life activities. Our tools were designed to collect this information from both parents and children. In this chapter we report on what parents wrote about the experience of their child. What support do they value for their child? In this chapter data from *both* phases of the study are examined, looking specifically at parents' responses to an open question that invited them to comment on the support that their child found helpful. The data are drawn from 5,432 completed questionnaires from 123 schools across England (71 primary, 28 secondary and 24 special schools) with pupils aged 2–19. Due to sampling procedures, there are more returns from pupils in year R (4–5 years), year 4 (8–9 years) and year 8 (12–13 years).

Children with an impairment or health condition

Taking the two studies together, 1,227 parents indicated that their child had a health condition or impairment – some 23 per cent of the questionnaires returned with a much lower proportion of the parents reporting that their child experienced a substantial impact on their participation in the activities of daily life – overall 9 per cent of the returns met the Equality Act criteria. As the previous chapter revealed, there was an uncertain relationship between impact and need, with a few children having a number of needs but parents reporting little impact. One possibility was that the impact of a child's impairment was offset by the support they received. This chapter includes the responses of both groups of parents – those who report both a high and a low impact. Taking only the substantial or high impact group would exclude valuable information about support from parents of those children who appeared to be benefiting most. Although the low impact group would probably not meet the Equality Act criteria, taking data about all children with a health condition or impairment provides important information about the ways in which schools can respond well to diversity. The data are reported by school phase to support this process.

Within the group of 1,227 children who had a health condition or impairment, 17 per cent had a diagnosis of ASD and 14 per cent of asthma, 13 per cent had mental health difficulties, 8 per cent of children had a visual impairment, 8 per cent a hearing impairment, 5 per cent had ADHD, 4 per cent epilepsy, and 2 per cent cerebral palsy. An overview of all parental comments is provided first before turning to the three largest groups – children who are on the autistic spectrum, children with asthma and children with mental health difficulties.

What support did parents say their child found helpful?

Parents were asked what support their child found particularly helpful and 732 parents of children with a health condition or impairment provided comments to this open question, 60 per cent of the sample. A higher proportion of parents who reported a substantial impact made comments – 78 per cent, compared to just 47 per cent of those parents whose child experienced low impact. An iterative process of data coding was adopted to reveal eight emergent categories: comments that concerned the organization for learning, notably reference to one-to-one support or small group learning; staff responses that communicated to the child positive understanding and being generally supportive; access to specialist advice both internal and external to the school; comments that related to the curriculum; mention of learning aids or resources; description of particular instructional approaches or styles; aspects of the environment including space and finally reference to particular medical or health related support.

Table 4.1 Parent responses – all children with a health condition or impairment

	Primary N=272	Secondary N=203	Special N=257	Total N=732
Organization for learning	75 (28%)	32 (16%)	77 (30%)	184 (25%)
Attitudes, understanding and being supportive	48 (18%)	39 (19%)	54 (21%)	141 (19%)
Specialist advice	47 (17%)	28 (14%)	65 (25%)	140 (19%)
Curriculum	43 (16%)	36 (18%)	32 (12%)	111 (15%)
Learning aids/equipment and resources	31 (11%)	19 (9%)	39 (15%)	89 (12%)
Instructional responses	48 (18%)	28 (14%)	29 (11%)	105 (14%)
Environment	19 (7%)	20 (10%)	20 (8%)	59 (8%)
Medical/health	75 (28%)	40 (20%)	11 (4%)	126 (17%)

Organization for learning

Looking across all phases of schooling, parents were most likely to mention aspects concerned with the organization for learning, namely individual support or the presence of a teaching assistant or rather less frequently being in a small group. This pattern was reflected in both primary and special school parent responses. In secondary school parents were more likely to mention having a teaching assistant supporting their child than the benefits of individual teaching or working in small groups. In special schools teaching assistants were much less frequently mentioned, with only a few parents stating that the presence of a teaching assistant was supportive compared to the more frequent reference to the importance of one-to-one teaching. Parents sometimes explained why their child found it helpful as these two quotes from secondary schools illustrate:

> Kit has told me he gets help from a class assistant. By having this help Kit is able to understand subject areas which he would otherwise find difficult. This person is also available for Kit to talk to if he has any other problems, ie. With other pupils.
>
> (Parent of a child in secondary school)

> She likes smaller groups as they are less noisy and she finds it easier to concentrate.
>
> (Parent of a child in secondary school)

And from primary schools:

> Support assistant is extremely important – enables/facilitates access to the curriculum, support with communication, equipment, emotional, social support.

> Working one to one he finds very helpful, especially if he's with someone he has clicked with.

And from a special school:

> For Martin to gain confidence and to understand things, he needs more time and patience in explaining things to him, one to one tuition with no distractions are a must for him to concentrate on the tasks at hand.

It is clear from these quotes that the organization for learning is not simply about access to the curriculum but also about the relationship with the person and this brings us to a second important theme.

Attitudes, understanding and being supportive

Just under one in five parents (19 per cent) wrote about the importance of staff attitudes towards their child. This was common to all three settings. Patience, understanding and reassurance were particular themes. They wanted staff to be sympathetic and understanding of their child's difficulties rather than judgemental.

> Acceptance and allowance for her special needs means that she is more relaxed, happy and confident in the classroom, and this will help her learning.
>
> (Parent of a child in primary school)

> Help when in difficulty. Not to feel that he is not good enough.
>
> (Parent of a child in secondary school)

> Elizabeth needs a lot of emotional support and reassurance.
>
> (Parent of a child in a special school)

Parents wanted staff to promote confidence and raise self-esteem and were particularly mindful of the impact when this did not happen.

> Elsa gets frustrated if she is not listened to when she has a problem. If people hurry her or get irritated this will exacerbate the situation and she will get upset and aggressive and anxious. General support, encouragement and understanding works wonders.
>
> (Parent of a child in primary school)

> Sometimes find difficult to take part in physical education because he feels tired and drained of energy. When sent a note to school to exclude him he was forced to join in and told 'if you are not well enough to do P.E. you should not be at school' the one time he collapsed after P.E. The hospital will be writing to the school.
>
> (Parent of a child in secondary school)

A few parents wrote about the importance of the school ethos being welcoming to diversity among pupils.

> Their school they attend is great. They have never been made to feel any different and have never had any difficulties to overcome. Their teachers have always been very understanding and supportive.
>
> (Parent of two children in primary school)

The school understands his limitations and accepts he cannot do rugby, they accept him just to get on with his everyday life and treat him as normal as all others.

(Parent of a child in secondary school)

They also commented on the importance of the teacher in communicating this to the children:

Teachers who help in a positive way to talk to class and other children in school about facial differences and psychologically support child if needed.

(Parent of a child in primary school)

The importance of staff understanding the child's difficulties is further emphasized by additional parents who did not write to explicitly identify support but provided comments to explain their child and their behaviours.

Chris copes mostly very well. It's the unknown or something new or different that can cause him to worry or become stressed. As sleeping is one of his major difficulties he is often exhausted and this can magnify things for him.

(Parent of child in secondary school)

Specialist advice

In addition to the attitudes of staff, unsurprisingly parents also valued specialist advice. One in four parents of children in special schools and one in six in primary and one in seven in secondary identified particular types of specialist who they had found helpful. These were a wide-ranging group including occupational, physio and speech therapists, consultants, dieticians and nurses, counsellors, social workers as well as specialist teaching staff. Speech therapists were the most frequently identified specialist to provide their child with support, especially for parents with children in primary and special schools:

He finds speech therapy very helpful because this would help him to talk and express his feelings and making other people understand him.

(Parent of a child in special school)

Aidan has help from the speech centre in (name of town). We have to take him out of school for this which is a concern and obviously they are very busy so he has block sessions.

(Parent of a child in primary school)

Parents also mentioned speech therapy as support from the past:

Only needed speech therapy when young – discharged – and the support was good.

> (Parent of a child in secondary school)

Through intensive speech therapy since the age of 30 months Colin's speech has improved dramatically. However he still struggles with some pronunciation and needs time to think and articulate himself. He needs to be allowed to finish his sentences and to let his train of thought be fully voiced, so time and patience are vital. Also an awareness by his classmates of their need to listen would perhaps improve his relationships?

> (Parent of a child in primary school)

Parents with children in secondary schools were more likely to mention specialists that provided counselling:

- Just started talking to school counsellor
- Waiting for appointment to see CAMS at (region) Hospital
- In regular contact with members of staff concerning panic/anxiety attacks.

> (Parent of a child in secondary school)

Doctors, nurses and paediatricians were also mentioned:

Becoming Diabetic has limited Danielle's activities during school sometimes if she has a hypo or feels unwell. Danielle has been a Type 1 Diabetic for 3 years. She finds helpful support from her family, friends, teachers, diabetic nurses, dietician and consultant paediatrician.

> (Parent of a child in primary school)

Specialist teachers were much more rarely mentioned, with only seven parents of children in primary schools, two in secondary and eight in special schools indicating that they found these professionals helpful. Even rarer were references to psychologists or social workers.

Parents included in their responses comments where specialist support was felt to be inadequate:

He does have speech and language therapy, but it's not every week, which is what he needs.

> (Parent of a child in primary school)

He has had no support at all. The people we have seen don't seem interested at anything I say. Apart from a paediatrician who diagnosed him with ADHD and I have seen two people since who have been no help at all.

> (Parent of a child in special school)

Instructional responses

Overall 14 per cent of parents wrote to suggest instructional strategies that supported their child's learning. Often their child found structure and routine particularly helpful – especially for those in special schools.

> Visual timetable; calm environment; consistency; understanding of sensory modulation dysfunction; self-calming strategies; confidence and self-esteem building strategies; TLC!
>
> (Parent of a child in special school)

> Everything has to be routine – if things change we have to let Tim know what is going to happen or where we are going. – Picture exchange cards have been very useful with helping Tim to talk and communicate.
>
> (Parent of a child in primary school)

Three other prominent themes included aspects of the way teachers communicated to pupils, especially from parents of children in primary school settings.

> Lily likes to be with the same people. She tends to 'bond' to people. She enjoys structure and routine. I attended an early birds course and was told to slow ones speech and repeat the same phrase. That seems to have brought her speech on no end.
>
> (Parent of a child in primary school)

A further theme that was cited by parents of children in mainstream education was providing encouragement and motivation:

> Milly is profoundly deaf – with a cochlear implant. As long as she is encouraged and pushed to do her best, she copes very well.
>
> (Parent of a child in primary school)

Parents also wrote about the importance of the child sitting at the front of the class or near the teacher:

> Sitting at the front of the class in a position of her choice so that she can accommodate her 'null point'. Clear diction. Consideration of the balance issues without excluding her from activities.
>
> (Parent of a child in secondary school)

Parents also made reference to the child needing more time to respond and a slower pace to the instruction and more repetition. A few also wrote about small steps or smaller targets. Some pupils clearly needed a range of particular instructional strategies.

Visual support, including demonstration and practise, mind-maps, pictures etc. Having his attention drawn to key points. Small class / group or individual teaching. Being seated in a position in the classroom where he won't be distracted and will be able to attend to teacher more easily (at the front?) Very hesitant about starting new things, joining groups so needs encouragement and preparation to ease the process. Specific anger management strategies positive reinforcement (any negative feedback has huge impact on self-esteem, anxiety, and increase negative behaviour).

(Parent of a child in secondary school)

Medical and health related support

In mainstream settings parents noted the importance of medical aspects of provision, i.e. support that would be provisioned outside the school setting, including medication, special diets and medical aids such as hearing aids. Overall 17 per cent of parents mentioned these, although notably this was unequally skewed towards mainstream settings, while parents in special schools by contrast rarely mentioned these as particular forms of support. The availability of medication and in particular the use of inhalers featured prominently amongst parent comments in both primary and secondary school returns.

Alex needs an inhaler on a regular basis. He has a normal healthy lifestyle otherwise and needs no extra support other than to be reassured that I'm there and he has access to his inhaler.

(Parent of a child in primary school)

Although much less frequent parents also cited particular appliances such as hearing aids and grommets. For a minority of parents the most important aspect was their child's diet, particularly where the child had an allergic reaction:

Severe eczema on back of leg – cream and antibiotics meant Cassi could use (stretch and bend) her leg without difficulty. Animal hair allergy – keeping away from cause of allergy but inhaler helps wheezing if there is contact.

(Parent of a child in secondary school)

For diabetic pupils regular monitoring was a vital part of the support:

Needs blood/sugar levels monitored and regular insulin injections.

(Parent of a child in primary school)

Learning aids and resources

In comparison to medical aids, school-based aids or resources were much less frequently mentioned, with one in eight (12 per cent) parents writing about some tangible aid. They were more likely to be mentioned by parents of children in special schools. Perhaps unsurprisingly computers were the most likely to be mentioned, although in some instances this also referred to working at the computer at home.

> Scribe in lessons and a reader parents scribe and read homework extra support/programmes to improve reading and writing abilities computer to help with work trying to set up dragon speaking friendly and other software to try and increase independence.
>
> (Parent of a child in secondary school)

> At school my child enjoys working on the computers. I understand he has a clear comprehension of the computer and of its many uses.
>
> (Parent of a child in special school)

Parents also wrote about low-tech support such as aids for reading:

> Blue or green paper not white. Black print moves around on paper.
>
> (Parent of a child in primary school)

> Cream paper, helpful, stops words moving about.
>
> (Parent of a child in secondary school)

Parents appreciated these low-tech, often non-commercial resources that were tailored to their child's interests and needs.

> He enjoys the games that are made for him, and the one to one tuition has been beneficial as its at his pace. But this is something he will struggle with all his life.
>
> (Parent of a child in special school)

Curriculum

Parents of children in secondary schools were slightly more likely to mention aspects of the curriculum than those in other settings with 18 per cent of these parents including reference to what was or should be taught to their child. Sixteen per cent of parents in primary schools and 12 per cent in special schools also referred to the content of teaching. Parents wrote about the need for both additional work in a particular area and alternatives or adapted work.

By far the most frequently mentioned area was reading or English, which was more than four times more likely to be cited than maths.

> Abigail has poor concentration. She is improving reading by attending extra classes promoting improvements to aid her problem in phonics. Abi does get lots of support but recently I have found her demanding attention more, has no patience.
>
> (Parent of a child in secondary school)

> It is mainly his handwriting and spelling. I make Stephan do handwriting practice at home, but I feel he needs more, cannot understand his writing sometimes.
>
> (Parent of a child in secondary school)

> Practice writing and reading regularly with teacher's aids (one to one) to aid fine and gross motor skills and communication skills.
>
> (Parent of a child in special school)

Parents also wrote about physical aspects of the curriculum and pupils needing alternatives to sport and PE. Perhaps surprisingly social skills were also mentioned, and usually by parents in primary and special school settings.

> The school offers a group session for him and others to discuss and learn about social skills. This is moderately helpful. He really just needs teachers to be understanding and on his side, most are not.
>
> (Parent of a child in primary school)

> School is really helping Charlie not only with his education but life skills as well i.e. feeding, drinking and toileting.
>
> (Parent of a child in special school)

Environment

The least frequently mentioned aspect of school support was the environment with only 8 per cent of parents directly noting this as being important for their child, with few differences between mainstream and special school returns. Where parents did mention it, reference was usually made to two elements, first that of noise and the acoustic properties of the environment and second that of providing a safe environment.

Noise was particularly an issue for pupils with a hearing impairment:

> Glue Ear – clear instructions that he can hear. It is difficult to hear over classroom noise or when he is in the playground. May seem he is ignoring you but does not hear all or part of instruction. Support – understanding

need, but not drawing attention to him, sit close to the teacher etc patience. Teacher who help in a positive way to talk to class and other children in school about facial differences and psychologically support child if needed.

(Parent of a child in primary school)

Because the school environment is noisy, Tyson needs to be spoken to face to face.

(Parent of a child in primary school)

Working in a quiet environment. Variety in learning methods.

(Parent of a child in primary school)

A few parents also mentioned the importance of a calm and predictable environment:

Calm and stress free environment. Needs a structured teaching environment and a flexible approach. Is making excellent progress in his special school.

(Parent of a child in special school)

Elizabeth needs a lot of emotional support and reassurance. Environment, activities, routines have to be kept in a certain order as change can cause distress and anxiety for Elizabeth.

(Parent of a child in special school)

Comments were made that linked aspects of a child's health condition to the properties of the physical environment. As a mother of a child in primary school wrote:

My child suffers from eczema and as a result finds it difficult to learn if the heating arrangements in the classroom are too high. Extremes of heat and cold cause great irritation, and therefore, distract. Keeping the environment (room) at an even temperature.

One strategy that teachers used which helped pupils access the environment was a pass card:

Pat has a pass-out card that when she needs to she may prepare to leave the school site at the end of the afternoon a little earlier than her peers to avoid being jostled, this has been most appreciated by Pat when her joints have been painful during a flare-up.

(Parent of a child in secondary school)

Despite the more limited number of comments by parents, the school environment, including the use of space and the physical properties of the environment, are clearly of vital importance for some children. If parents spend little sustained time in school they may be less aware of the extent to which this impacts on their child.

We now turn to look briefly at targeted groups within the data: children with ASD, the majority of who were in special school provision, pupils with asthma, the majority of whom were in mainstream education, and lastly those with mental health conditions.

Children with autistic spectrum disorder

The most common diagnosis that children received was that of autistic spectrum disorder, and the data were analyzed to investigate whether, as previous writers have found, there were issues that were specific to this group. Of the 206 with this diagnosis, the majority of children (69 per cent) were educated in special schools, with 20 per cent in primary and 11 per cent in secondary schools. Taking the group as a whole, over 90 per cent experienced difficulties participating in classroom learning and interacting with peers. Indeed four in five parents reported that the condition limited activities at home. The breadth of the impact is a notable feature of this group. Most parents (83 per cent) rated the impact of their child's condition as substantial with only 16 per cent experiencing a minor impact to participation in daily life activities. Over 80 per cent of the parents made comments about what their child found helpful with the largest category of comments falling within the organization for learning category with 40 per cent of parents making comments concerning the benefit for their child having one to one or small group learning or being supported by a classroom assistant.

> 1-1 or small group support in all areas of curriculum. – Pre-tutoring of all areas of expectations to ease anxiety. – Social stories.
>> (Parent of a child in primary school)

> One to one support at school, clear routine and instructions, structured day, continued re-affirment of behaviour and expectations. Computer access at school and home. One to one support to access music tuition, gym.
>> (Parent of a child in special school)

The second most frequent category of response was instructional responses, with 22 per cent of parents overall mentioning aspects of pedagogy. This was particularly true for parents of children in primary schools where two in three parents commented on a preferred teaching approach.

Table 4.2 Parent responses – children with autistic spectrum disorder

Parents' comments on support	Primary N=34	Secondary N= 20	Special N= 117	Total N=171
Organization for learning	21	5	42	68 (40%)
Attitudes, understanding and being supportive	5	4	23	32 (19%)
Specialist advice	9	4	18	31 (18%)
Curriculum	8	4	14	26 (15%)
Aids and resources	6	2	17	25 (15%)
Instructional responses	15	6	17	38 (22%)
Environmental	4	1	10	15 (9%)
Medication/diet/medical aids	2	2	4	8 (5%)

> ADULTS TO UNDERSTAND ASD ie no point asking Jordan to stop doing something if request is directed to whole class/group. He needs HIS name called followed by request/instruction. ADULTS to be aware of Jordan's triggers and to understand his inappropriate responses are very difficult for him to curb. ADULTS to be aware how other pupils treat him i.e. he is their 'pet' in order to be accepted, teased because of his extreme response.
>
> (Parent of a child in primary school)

This was the largest category of response for parents with children in secondary schools although their responses were distributed thinly across categories:

> Clear short instructions. Really needs someone to organise him.
>
> (Parent of a child in secondary school)

In common with the larger group, attitudes and understanding were mentioned by just under one in five parents, one parent indicating the importance of the school ethos:

> A school ethos that actually welcomes disability diversities.
>
> (Parent of a child in primary school)

Parents noted a diverse range of specialists that were supporting their child and in a few instances supporting the family as a whole:

> We have a group family therapy with a specialist Asd therapist monthly, we have star charts and reward charts. She has 1-1 support with some subjects at school, we try to get her to attend homework club at school. She is supervised and accompanied on many of her outside curriculum activities.
>
> (Parent of a child in secondary school)

The child has had invaluable support from social worker who has arranged short term breaks and access to home support from a local agency to help with life skills and educational needs. The input from psychologist to access behavioural needs. Child has had support from others such as doctors, to meet medical needs.

(Parent of a child in special school)

While this group therefore had much in common with the larger group, organization for learning and instructional responses stand out as particular areas of support.

Health needs

Some 680 children had a health condition and no reported learning difficulty. Most of these, 85 per cent, experienced no substantial impact on their daily life. The largest group of children with a health condition were the children with asthma. In total 272 children had asthma varying from mild to more significant (144 in primary schools, 123 in secondary and just six in special schools) and the majority (80 per cent) had no additional needs. Fewer than 15 per cent experienced difficulty participating in school or home activities. For many of the children the impact of their health condition caused no difficulty and where it did it combined with additional difficulties that the child experienced. It is therefore unsurprising that fewer parents, 44 per cent, provided comments on what their child found supportive and that when they did the most commonly referred to support was medical in nature, with just over half commenting often to refer to the importance of the child having access to their inhaler:

When Joseph becomes breathless he needs to have his inhaler straight away. I have to give Joseph his inhaler twice a day at home, but when his chest is bad he has to have it more often. Joseph suffers from chest infections about every 5/6 weeks so when his chest is bad he needs his inhaler at school.

(Parent of a child in primary school)

Asthma – mild. Uses Preventer daily. Uses blue inhaler as required and before exercise. Wayne self-administers. Sometimes feels he under performs in PE and on playground.

(Parent of a child in secondary school)

Taking all the children with asthma, attitudes and understanding are mentioned by 13 per cent of parents. As one parent of a child in a secondary school stated:

- P.E. teacher showing understanding of problem – asthma
- Understanding that school absence is sometimes unavoidable.

Table 4.3 Parent responses – children with asthma

Parents' comments on support	Primary N=65	Secondary N=49	Special N=6	Total N=120
Organization for learning	3	I	I	5
Attitudes, understanding and being supportive	5	6	4	15 (13%)
Specialist advice	4	3	0	7
Curriculum	8	3	I	12 (10%)
Learning aids and resources	4	3	I	8
Instructional responses	2	2	I	5
Environmental	2	2	I	5
Medication/diet/medical aids	41	27	0	68 (57%)

And another parent similarly says:

> Not being made to take part in sports if asthma present.
>
> (Parent of a child in secondary school)

Additionally, 12 parents also mentioned aspects of the curriculum: five of these concerned supporting maths or English or both but the remainder referred to additional or alternative approaches to the curriculum:

> Having missed periods of 2–3 weeks at a time my daughter would benefit from extra help to 'catch-up' the time she has missed either in classroom support or extra work at home relating to the period she has missed.
>
> (Parent of an eight-year-old girl in primary school)

> Alternatives to outdoor play, physical activities when in recouperation.
>
> (Parents of a seven-year-old girl in primary school)

These comments illustrate the important role for all school staff in being aware of the child's health needs, not simply those who take the pupils for sporting activities.

Mental health difficulties

The place of mental health in relation to disability is not straightforward, and this is particularly true with reference to children and young people. In total there were 156 children whose parents identified them as having mental health needs, 83 in mainstream provision and 73 in special schools, but not all of these children would be identified using the Equality Act criteria. Parents reported a substantial impact for 108 (69 per cent) of the pupils, 44 of whom were in mainstream education. These included children with depression, anxiety and phobias. An additional five children in mainstream education were clearly at risk of falling within this category and they were either seeing a counsellor or waiting for an appointment.

This group included many children who struggled to participate in classroom learning and/or interacting with their peers (78 per cent) and for the majority in joining in other school activities (74 per cent). Slightly fewer experienced difficulties at home (62 per cent). Seventy-one per cent of parents reported that their child experienced a substantial impact on daily life as a result of their difficulties. Only 20 children had no additional needs identified by their parents. Around 70 per cent of the pupils in primary and special schools also had a behavioural difficulty, but this was only reported to be the case by 43 per cent of secondary school parents. Around 70 per cent also had a learning difficulty and just over half speech and language difficulties. Many of these children had a complex array of needs.

Just over three-quarters of the parents (76 per cent) wrote about what their child found helpful.

Table 4.4 presents an overview of the comments made by parents of children with mental health needs. This was a diverse group of children as many had a range of needs, and parents did not always explicitly address mental health needs when they wrote about what their child found helpful. Taking these two cautions in mind, parents were slightly more likely to highlight both the importance of organizational factors as well as attitudes and understanding of staff.

> Non-intrusive support, so that he has a person he can 'run' to when he is likely to lose control. He responds well to encouragement, boosting his self-esteem which otherwise is very low, therefore he needs support that provides this positive feedback.
>
> (Parent of a child in primary school)

> 1:1 support for all activities routine. Non-judgemental attitude from adults too could bridge the division between his world and other peoples. Specialist rather than mainstream educational/social support.
>
> (Parent of a child in special school)

Table 4.4 Parent responses – all children with mental health needs

Parents' comments on support	Primary N=31	Secondary N=33	Special N=55	Total N=119
Organization for learning	11	5	17	33 (28%)
Attitudes, understanding and being supportive	5	11	16	32 (27%)
Specialist advice	6	5	11	22 (18%)
Curriculum	4	1	6	11 (9%)
Learning aids and resources	2	7	9	18 (15%)
Instructional responses	10	5	11	26 (22%)
Environmental	2	2	6	10 (8%)
Medication/diet/ medical aids	4	6	3	13 (11%)

In secondary school settings the attitude and understanding of others were particularly important whereas in primary schools more reference was made to access to one-to-one support and being in small groups.

> Skilled Teaching Assistant really helps Michael get through a day at school. He has occasionally received counselling, which was beneficial, and advice from a psychiatrist. Michael ... becomes emotional quite easily and so I am glad of any support I can get.
>
> (Parent of a boy in secondary school)

Flexibility in the responsiveness of school was also important:

> Pacing in relation to physical activities and mental activities ... Support from friends. Consideration of timescales for homework. Consideration of periods of absence. (Alice currently takes Thursdays off, but has often taken further days off due to extreme fatigue). Being allowed to stay in class breaks, enter dinner hall early.
>
> (Parent of a 14-year-old girl in secondary school)

A number of parents made reference to counselling although specialist services were not always viewed positively:

> Helen has seen CAMHS for several years, also the school psychologist, counsellors and a family support worker, none of which she found helpful.
>
> (Parent of a 13-year-old girl in secondary school)

Many children, especially those with the most complex needs, require an array of support:

> Tim needs lots of support to get along with his teachers and accept direction. Tim needs support to understand communication with friends, to control his behaviour and reduce anxiety. Tim is very upset at school and hates his teacher, he needs lots of support to deal with this. Tim receives mental health support via psychologists, psychotherapy and psychiatry. He is often very depressed and talks about ending his life. Tim needs support when out and about to reduce anxiety and stay safe (noise, unexpected change etc). Tim needs to control his asthma and migraines with medication which gets worse with anxiety, allergies and stress. Lots of adult support needed.
>
> (Parent of a 12-year-old boy in special school)

This quote illustrates the ways in which different conditions interrelate and require sensitive and informed interactions from others. The responses from parents demonstrate some of the challenges pupils face:

Luke has had a rough time, in terms of divorce, cafcass reports, court cases
and a lot of deaths in the family.

(Parent of a child in primary school)

And the important role of school as well as other professionals in supporting
pupils:

Open access to paediatric ward of local hospital community medical
personnel – nurses, carers, telephone contact with paediatricians. Regular
respite with childrens hospices. Sympathetic and understanding personnel
at school. Regular attendance at school.

(Parent of a child in special school)

Implications of the data

The parent responses reflected the range of challenges children experience
from those which occur regularly in every setting to those which are only
occasionally experienced. However a common factor that united the children
was the effect on classroom life and in consequence the pivotal role to be
played by schools to enable their full participation in daily activities. Despite
the diversity across the group the greatest area of support was seen in the way
that learning was organized and in particular the child's contact with adults.
Overall a quarter of parents wrote that this was an aspect that was important for
their child, especially for those in primary and special school settings. Access to
adults featured heavily in parental responses with a quarter specifically referring
to individual support, small groups or small classes. Parents saw this form of
organization as essential for the child's learning. This requirement was often
linked in parent comments to providing a positive emotional climate, one
where staff gave encouragement and reassurance.

While schools may view the organization for learning as a pedagogic response
there is also a relational or affective element. Research has raised some important
questions about the efficacy of support provided by classroom assistants in one-
to-one and small group settings in mainstream schools (Webster et al. 2010). A
longitudinal UK study of everyday provision in schools revealed that teachers
were almost entirely engaged in whole-class work in both primary and
secondary settings and that it was teaching assistants (TAs) who provided small
group and individual support. The data suggest that this had a negative impact
on pupil progress in core subjects even when controlling for factors such as
prior attainment and SEN status (Blatchford et al. 2009), as TAs lacked the
pedagogical skills to promote pupil understanding. Instead their focus was on
task completion, prompting pupils even by supplying the answers. Where TAs
are trained to deliver a highly structured programme the outcomes are more
promising (Farrell et al. 2010).

Given that parental comments less frequently referred to other elements of pedagogical support, it is possible that their view of the supportive nature of these organizational arrangements reflects additional values. Howes *et al.* (2003), in a review of previous research, suggest that the style of interactions of a TA is different to that of a teacher and more likely to be informal and personalized, helping pupils to engage and stay on task. Webster *et al.* (2010) refer to this as developing the 'soft skills – confidence and motivation, dispositions towards learning' (p. 331), and this was reflected in our data. Given the personalized and more extended interaction that TAs have with pupils it is quite possible that this increased interest and attention is what parents value, and they, like others, are not aware that this does not necessarily lead to improved learning outcomes but do see it as important for their child's wellbeing.

Consistent with this analysis is the finding that in secondary schools there was a slight shift in parental responses to focus on the nature of the relationships children have with adults, whether they are understanding and supportive in their attitude towards the child. Notably this was also cited as an aspect that created barriers for the child. Research has consistently addressed the importance of attitudes in promoting the inclusion of children with disability and SEN in school life, and 'being helpful' can be as important as the help received. One way in which parents promoted a more positive attitude was by providing explanations of *why* particular support was helpful, often relating this to the child's specific needs. This was also reflected in parents' comments that access to specialist advice was helpful, providing knowledge and understanding of children's particular difficulties. Parsons *et al.* (2009b) also refer to the 'strong desire for children's individual needs to be adequately recognized, understood and supported' (p. 54), although they conclude that equally important is the knowledge and understanding of the 'impact of different conditions, disorders, disabilities or difficulties on children's individual experiences and capabilities' (p. 54). The emphasis here can be placed on pupils' experiences and wellbeing rather than on a more narrowly conceived view of attainment. Notably parental comments about the curriculum were often about providing opportunities for children to develop their self-esteem and self-confidence, to promote their social and communicative skills rather than to address particular areas of academic knowledge. The exception were comments with respect to improving children's reading and writing skills, ones that would be needed to access the wider curriculum.

Parents also wrote about the resources and equipment that supported pupils' learning. Although many mentioned computers, many of the resources were low-tech, ones that had been devised with the particular needs of the individual child in mind. From a school's perspective the development of these aids requires a little time and specialist knowledge rather than financial investment. One resource that was particularly useful was that of a pass, enabling the child to access a facility or be absent from a lesson, legitimizing being treated differently.

Relatively few parents wrote about the environment, although when they did this was often an essential part of enabling pupils to participate fully. One particular group were children with hearing loss for whom background noise was an important factor in enabling them to take a full part in school activities. However it is likely that acoustic properties of a classroom impact more widely on children's ability to concentrate. Tufvesson and Tufvesson (2009) review the evidence on how sound and light levels impact on disabled children's ability to concentrate and their behaviour. Others have written about the positioning of windows and doors, the storage of equipment, the wall displays and it is possible that when parents write about the importance of a calm environment they are also alluding to these aspects. For pupils with allergies ventilation and heating are also important.

Within the data are hidden the needs of different groups. In this chapter I have drawn out contrasts between pupils with ASD, pupils with asthma and those with mental health difficulties, three conditions which are increasing in prevalence. Notably parents of children with ASD and those with mental health difficulties were particularly forthcoming about the support needs of their child. Previous research on parents of children with ASD has highlighted the factors that appear to be associated with parental levels of satisfaction with the educational provision of their child. Whitaker (2007) writes:

> The extent to which parents felt that school staff understood (and empathised) with their children's difficulties, and the perceived flexibility of the schools' responses to the children's needs ... The extent and quality of reciprocal communication between school and home [were] strongly associated with levels of satisfaction.
>
> (p. 170)

The data here support this conclusion.

Two additional groups that were identified are children whose needs may be invisible to the school, often because they vary across time and context. The numbers of children diagnosed with asthma has been increasing over the past 20 years (Wolf et al. 2008). Unsurprisingly medical support is the highest reported form of support for those with asthma (and low for those with ASD), as parents stress the importance of children having access to their inhalers and being able to self-medicate. While the evidence of effectiveness is not clear-cut, self-management is an important strategy for children with asthma (Wolf et al. 2008). However there are also important reminders in the data that health needs can generate the need for other educational responses. Asthmatic children for example may also require curriculum adjustments, partly due to absences that mean they may need the opportunity to catch up on learning that they have missed.

Children with mental health needs are also a growing group (Nuffield Foundation 2012) with a doubling in the last 30 years of the number of young people who report that they frequently feel anxious or depressed. Where children have additional difficulties, it may be particularly challenging to recognize these needs (Hackett *et al.* 2010) and it's likely that the returns under-represented this group. This group included a number of parents who were waiting for appointments with professionals, uncertain whether their child had a significant health need or not. As one parent wrote, 'it could just be her turning into a teenager'. The data that was provided however illustrate finely the need for schools to be supportive and to provide an environment that does not exacerbate the challenges the child faces. There was a plea by some parents to look beyond the behaviour to understand what may lie beneath it. Again the emphasis on being part of a smaller classroom unit and having access to a teaching assistant speak not just of a pedagogic response to the way that learning is organized, but also of the desire for a closer relationship, one which is flexible and responsive to children's changing needs.

However the data also revealed some ambivalence about the schools and professional involvement with some parents being concerned that their child's mental health difficulty should not be discussed. Schools therefore have a sensitive role to play in providing genuine opportunities for parents to contribute to enabling their child to participate fully in school life. It is likely that the 'reasonable adjustments' that parents want are first and foremost to understand the needs of their child. Where absence plays a key part in the child's coping, staff may be unaware of the challenges they face in participating in school life. While local authorities assess their services for children with mental health difficulties as high, including those for children with learning difficulties (DfE 2011b), the data from parents suggest that everyday contact with understanding adults within the school has a vital role to play in supporting their child.

These findings are highly consistent with research on the social dimensions of schooling and the impact of relationships with teachers and others on a pupil's sense of wellbeing. McLaughlin and Clarke (2010) review a body of research that reveals the interconnectedness of learning, relating and belonging. Particularly relevant here is the evidence that teachers who are 'good', and in particular perceived as kind and supportive, play a particular role in emotional wellbeing, an example of the way you are treated being as important as how well you are taught. To understand these experiences we need to learn from the children themselves and the following chapter provides an analysis of children's responses across the three phases of schools that took part in the study.

Chapter 5

What data tell us about children's experiences

Introduction

Parents provide one perspective on the experiences of children with a health condition or impairment but they may provide limited information on how the child encounters barriers and supports to participation in everyday life. Capturing children's views is therefore fundamental to gaining a fuller understanding of the experience of disability. This however is not without challenges and much has been written elsewhere about gaining the authentic voice of the child, including that of the disabled young person (Beresford 2012; Bragg 2007; Christensen and James 2008; Lewis 2011; Porter 2014). These don't simply concern how to find an appropriate mode of communication or supporting children in recalling, but more subtle influences at work that reflect power imbalances that are prevalent in school organization and structures. Just as we recognize the ways in which the environment shapes the experience of an impairment or health condition so too we need to recognize the impact of the context on the views that are expressed and the voices that are heard. The natural corollary to this is that using a range of methods, flexibly, in different settings can offset some of these challenges. Schools where there is an ethos of listening to children are better placed to gather knowledge that supports an understanding of children's experiences. In these environments children are more likely to expect to be heard.

There are compelling arguments for adopting an inclusive approach to the collection of these views, one which ensures that *all* children contribute to making schools better places for learning. Gathering the views of only known disabled children is likely to ignore the needs of some children who are struggling. A message that has been repeated in the book is that it is likely that schools don't know about the difficulties experienced by some disabled children, indeed they may be unaware of the existence of a medical condition or impairment, especially where these are cyclical and hidden from view through absences from school or well-honed self-management strategies.

The tools and guidance that were developed for this project therefore reflected concerns to meet the communication needs of *all* children, recognizing the ways in which barriers can be erected through choice of presentation and response modes. We included structured and more open methods, recognizing that pre-selection of vocabulary determines the possibility of meanings. For example, the availability of particular symbols or the range of response options limits what it is possible and permissible to say. Equally pupils can be hindered by the cognitive demands of recalling events, people and places that are distant in time and space. Any parent who has been met with silence following the question 'what did you do in school today?' can recognize the universality of this challenge. Supporting devices, whether visual, tangible or conversational, are needed. Communicating one's views can also be an emotional activity, and children need to know that their ideas will be valued and taken seriously. Comments on the parent questionnaire suggest that this does not happen for some young people. We were also mindful that both staff and pupils may need support in being encouraged to reflect, and sometimes at length, on negative experiences that surface as barriers to participation.

The research team therefore developed activities that could be used with small and larger groups of children, including whole classes, mindful that this encouraged teachers and all children to engage in discussions of what supported learning and be more aware of others' needs. An emphasis was placed on the introduction to activities so that they were couched in discussion of valuing difference and acknowledgement that everybody faces challenges in life, things that they find a bit tricky. Activities were also targeted at different ages so that even the youngest children were introduced to thinking and talking about barriers and supports to participation in schools.

Group activities did not totally replace the need for individual methods however. Children with significant communication, cognitive and emotional needs often require tailor-made approaches. Additionally, while group settings can be more fun, and the presence of friends or peers can give confidence and help children recall, others can find it difficult to take turns, or get impatient or angry with others. An individual setting can provide the time and space to talk about more private or potentially embarrassing things and without the possibility of being interrupted or judged by one's peers. To meet these varying needs six different approaches were developed and piloted working alongside teachers before being offered more widely to schools in both phases of the project. The developmental stage informed both the testing of the activity but also enabled the guidance for schools to be honed. The activities were described as 'flexible' tools – ones that could be adapted by schools, although the degree to which they were structured varied. They included:

1   Good and Bad Things About School: this was based on the approach adopted by Talking Mats (Cameron and Murphy 2002) that uses a simple symbol array to enable young people to record the barriers/things that make school difficult and the things that help them in school by placing pictures of activities, people and places alongside a symbol that best represents their feeling, good, bad or uncertain.

2   Symbol Questionnaire: this questionnaire was designed by members of the research team in collaboration with Widgit symbols to find out about aspects of school life for pupils who find both verbal communication and reading text difficult. It has been designed to be fully editable so that it can be tailored to match the experiences and interests of the individual child. Through the use of symbols it explores what children think about different times in the school day, different lessons, and asks whether they find it difficult to get around, do work, be with grown-ups, make friends, play with others, go to the toilet or travel on the bus or taxi. It asks them what they think about working on their own, with their teacher/support worker, and with other children. It also asks what would make school better.

3   Point to Point: this tool was based around counselling techniques and provides a concrete approach focusing on specific events that the child identifies as good or bad. With the help of a facilitator pupils represent these events with a mark on paper to locate when they felt best and when they felt worst. They then position themselves on a line between the best and worst indicating how they feel today. This activity provides a vehicle for exploring the barriers that contributed to the worst and the positive supports that contributed to the best experiences.

4   Younger Child Interview Schedule: this was designed to be undertaken either individually or in a small group and starts by exploring children's favourite things about school as well as those aspects they don't like doing. It asks if there is anything about the rooms, the playground, the toilets, or lesson times that make things difficult and what would make it easier. It asks if there is anything about the way people talk to them, about the journey to and from school and about moving around school that makes it difficult and again what would make it easier.

5   Focus Group using Nominal Group Technique: this structured method for group 'thought showering' encouraged contributions from everyone, which were then narrowed down through discussion. Every member of the group then ranked them via a voting system. Suggested questions around which to discuss included: *What gets in the way to getting on well in school? What support would help to get around these barriers?*

6   Online Questionnaire: also available in hard copy form, this had both open and closed questions. It invited pupils to rate their experiences in school at different times and places and also in the classroom during different types and organization of lessons. It asked what helped in those activities and what made them more difficult. It also asked if they had a disability or difficulty and if this had gone on for a long time.

Guidance for staff was developed and representatives from each school in the project were invited to a briefing meeting to facilitate schools' understanding of the ethos that underpinned the use of the tools. We emphasized the importance of children being invited to take part in the activities, rather than assuming their participation and for staff to be sensitive to children looking uncomfortable and responding in a way that suggested that they did not wish to take part, developing what Skånfors (2009) would refer to as an ethical radar. Guidance was given for choosing between the activities, giving examples of time length, group size, etc. Suggestions were made for introducing the activity and setting ground rules, for recording and acting on the information and for embedding the activity within the curriculum.

Table 5.1 reveals schools' choice and use of the flexible tools across the three sectors, with much higher usage of those tools which required relatively little preparation.

Interestingly when we introduced a symbol questionnaire that could be edited, following feedback from schools in the initial phases of the study its use declined. On the one hand schools appeared to favour more structured approaches – those which might be judged as most efficient – as not only did they take less time to prepare but they could be used with larger numbers of children. In some instances therefore rather than carry out the interview as a discussion, schools chose to convert the questions to written format, making it more easily administered to larger groups of children and providing them with a written record. The timelines for the study may well have contributed to their selection criteria.

Project data were returned to the team by the schools for further analysis and unsurprisingly this was most comprehensive for the structured tools and it is these that are reported on more fully here. The following section summarizes the data received for the talking mats, the symbol questionnaire, point to point, the structured focus groups and online questionnaire. Examples are given of the ways in which the schools used and adapted these approaches. The data were generated with the intention that they would be used at school level, enabling staff to consider what children found helpful and what barriers were experienced at both the level of the group and at that of the individual child. It was hoped therefore that they would both aggregate and disaggregate the data, facilitating changes at whole school level as well as where appropriate specifically for an individual pupil. In this report, where it is feasible, we look for issues that appear to be prominent across settings, and changes that

Table 5.1 School use of the flexible tools

Numbers of schools using	Primary	Secondary	Special	Total
Talking mats	11	0	2	13
Symbol questionnaire	8	1	13	22
Point to point	3	0	0	3
Interview schedule	10	2	7	19
Focus group	4	1	0	5
Online questionnaire	18	12	1	31

commonly appear with age. At points it is possible to compare the experiences of disabled children with their peers, drawing out both similarities and differences.

We turn first to the tool used with the youngest children, moving through the tool use by average age of the child – although notably the last to be described, the online questionnaire, was widely used across both primary and secondary settings.

Good and bad things about school

This approach was designed for children who expressed their views through a combination of symbols and pictures. Teachers however also selected to use these with children who were not confident communicators. With both groups it was useful to introduce the activity by asking children about their favourite foods or other items where it was clear that what was being asked for was the child's opinion, and counter the tendency of pupils to check that they had the 'right' answer. This also enabled staff to introduce the category of 'unsure', where pupils had no firm view either way. Many of the examples sent to us did not contain this mid-position symbol, and it is unclear whether this is because the children did not understand or because staff did not realize the significance of not being forced to have a view, that an aspect of school experience could be neither liked nor disliked. One alternative approach adopted by a teacher in a primary school circumvented these difficulties. Working with two pupils aged four, she gave out counters depicting like and dislike and invited the children to place them in turn on photographs of activities, places and people, enabling pupils to place symbols against those aspects which they felt strongly about, rather than being forced to have an opinion. Reports from teachers indicate that the activity did help them to identify locations and times of the day that children did not like. Canteens and toilets featured in the examples given, with staff learning that noise, such as banging doors, made them scary places for young children.

Some schools used this activity across a whole class and in one primary school the three reception class teachers took their own photographs, of five different environments, five activities and four groups of staff. Together they used the activity in a one-to-one setting with 76 children asking them their opinions on these different aspects of school to see what was liked or disliked and why. Children's responses were recorded on three A4 class response sheets for each aspect allowing them to track individual as well as shared aspects.

As we have found elsewhere children are more likely to express like and this is reflected here with 50 per cent of the children liking all five environments, over 60 per cent liking all five activities and 74 per cent liking all four sets of people. However there were also a few children for whom the opposite was true. Staff were able to ask children why they disliked or liked different aspects, revealing that young children at least found it difficult to comment on people

Table 5.2 Good and bad things about school: children's responses to photographs

Number of photos liked	5	4	3	2	1	0	Number of children responding	Number of children commenting
Environment	50%	29%	14%	5%	1%	0	76	34
Activities	61%	30%	4%	4%	1%	0	77	39
People	n/a	74%	5%	17%	4%	0	76	4

but were more able to talk about different activities and environments. The activity revealed children's growing awareness of feeling different or findings things difficult. For nine children this included PE, either because of getting changed, 'some people stare at me', or because they found it physically difficult: 'it makes my legs hurt'.

Symbol questionnaire

Thirteen schools returned data using the symbol questionnaire, four primary schools used it with 110 children and nine special schools with 166 children. Data from the two groups of children were largely similar. The majority of children thought school was good or at least OK with around one in ten children in both settings rating it as bad.

Table 5.3 Data from the symbol questionnaire: what children think about school

1. What do you think about school?	Bad	Good	OK
Primary (N=110)	9%	61%	29%
Special (N=166)	10%	63%	27%

When asked about school activities, assemblies were disliked by many children in both settings and this was only eclipsed in primary schools by responses to circle time. Conversely few children disliked break and dinner time. Fewer special school children didn't like home time (5 per cent) compared to primary (15 per cent).

Table 5.4 Data from the symbol questionnaire: what children don't like about school

3. At school I DON'T like:	Primary N=110	Special N=166
Assembly	28%	29%
Break	11%	9%
Circle	36%	27%
Dinner time	13%	11%
Home time	15%	5%

When asked about what they find difficult in school, children were most likely to indicate that doing work was difficult with around three in ten pupils indicating this. Children also indicated that they found the social aspects of playing with others and making friends difficult, and this was particularly true of primary school pupils where between one in four and one in five found these activities difficult.

Table 5.5 Data from the symbol questionnaire: what children find difficult about school

6. At school it is difficult to...	Primary N=110	Special N=166
Get around	9%	15%
Go to the toilet	13%	18%
Play games	21%	17%
Do work	29%	30%
Play with others	27%	27%
Make friends	27%	21%
Be with grown ups	17%	15%
Travel on the minibus or taxi	5%	14%

Children were also asked what they thought about different ways of working and children were more likely to respond that they disliked working by themselves, especially in primary schools (57 per cent), but this was also indicated by many special school pupils (33 per cent). As one might anticipate, however, a proportion (14 per cent primary and 18 per cent special) disliked working with other children.

Children were also asked what would make school better, what they would like more help with. In special schools the most frequent response was work, where 36 per cent of children would like more support. This compares to 25 per cent of the primary school children. In both cases this is quite a significant response. However a higher request by primary school pupils was help with making friends where 59 per cent of pupils would like support and 29 per cent of special school pupils.

We were particularly interested to interrogate the data in the light of other research suggesting that children might find it difficult to disagree with statements and to indicate areas that they didn't like. Within the special

Table 5.6 Data from the symbol questionnaire: what children dislike about working

Do you dislike	Primary N=110	Special N=166
Working by yourself?	57%	33%
Working with other children?	14%	18%
Working with the teacher?	10%	9%
Working with your helper/support worker?	12%	12%

school population, two pupils said they didn't like anything except home time, a consistent set of responses. This was also the profile of one young pupil in primary who disliked everything but home time. A minority of pupils made seemingly discrepant responses. In the special school population, one child said they both liked and disliked special days and three similarly responded with respect to assemblies and one to circle time. In the primary school population, two children said they both liked and disliked dinner time and home time and one responded similarly with respect to break time. It may be that all these respondents really needed a category of response which enabled them to respond that 'sometimes' they disliked and liked a particular context. As with all these tools, they indicate that these summary statements require some follow-up to find out more. For example staff might take the data as a cue to be particularly vigilant to what is happening for particular pupils at disliked times of the day.

Example of how one school used the symbol questionnaire

An all-age special school was using a wide range of flexible tools to find out the views of all pupils on things that help and things that make life more difficult. The class teacher decided that the best approach for one year 4 pupil with learning difficulties might be for him to complete the questionnaire at home with his parents and bring back it into school. She talked to both parents, emphasizing the importance of getting Daniel's own views and they were keen to be involved. This approach worked; separating the activity from the school surroundings helped to make it seem more purposeful, as Daniel was completing the questionnaire with people who didn't already know the answer to the questions. They identified an area of difficulty in travelling in the minibus, which was investigated further. It transpired than Daniel did not like to lose sight of his bag during the journey and arrangements were put in place to get around this problem. The class teacher suggested to parents that they might like to keep a set of symbols at home to use from time to time, to help Daniel express his views more readily and take a fuller part in annual reviews.

Point to point

Schools were least likely to choose the point to point activity, possibly because it required a specific focus on a particular event that a pupil had found very difficult, and as one teacher told us they did not feel well prepared to do this. It was also likely to be an activity that staff were less familiar with, given its origination in counselling. However one school embraced it with all classes using it with a total of 48 pupils, all of whom were described as having emotional, social and behavioural difficulties and a researcher was fortunate enough to be present on these occasions.

The deputy head of this special school introduced the activity in a school assembly where the pupils had started to think about their best and worst days at school, things that can get in the way and things that can support learning. The teacher then followed it up with a small group of pupils who were used to working together. He prompted the pupils to think about school by using an example from his own school life. He said one of the most important and best days was when he realized he could read on his own.

Pupils were then given an A3 sheet of paper with 'My best day' at the top, with a box for a picture and six bubbles for them to write in. In the lower half of the paper, 'My worst day' was written. There were four bubbles for negative factors and a box to draw a picture. There was a line down the right-hand side. The issues raised by the children included doing something they regretted, being bullied and friends going away. The teacher supported the pupils to think through the issues, reflecting back their comments and feelings and gently asking questions that help to identify sources of support and strategies, e.g. was there anybody who could have helped? How would you like to have done? What would you do now if you were in that position?

The activity was brought to a close by the teacher commenting that some things can stay with you for a long time and that you often remember things that you didn't like happening. He said that their ideas may change with time.

Notably, in another group, a teacher explained the activity by adding 'I don't mean ordinary bad, things that make for a horrible day', which produced rather more significant responses:

- punching my cousin;
- when I heard my mum was going to die;
- going to the dentist and having teeth taken out;
- being shouted at by teachers;
- being blamed for something I didn't do.

Looking across the data from that special school, the children gave 82 descriptions of the worst day – many individuals had more than one. Perhaps unsurprisingly in this group, pupils wrote about aspects of interaction experienced by themselves or inflicted by others. The pupils were slightly more likely to talk about themselves and their behaviour (35 per cent) than they were about interactions with others (27 per cent), writing about being spat at and pushed, screaming and kicking as well as difficult phonecalls home. Friends did not explicitly feature very often (4 per cent) and nor did family (6 per cent). While one in five wrote about major events, often involving coping with change (first day at school, death of family members, birthdays and

Christmas), others referred to things that were disruptive to routines such as late taxis or buses, late breaks, arriving late in school. Aspects of school work (tests, lessons, reading and writing) were mentioned by 20 per cent of pupils. A small number (7 per cent) wrote about sanctions, usually using break or playtime, and the same number referred to aspects of the environment, noise, temperature, etc.

The school revealed for us the different ways in which worst and best days might be interpreted by children. For some there are highly poignant events that mark out a particular day while for others their days are coloured by more frequently occurring phenomena that are often experienced as outside the control of the young person.

Nominal group technique

We turn now to the use of the specialized form of structured focus group. Although four primary schools used it as part of the project we did not receive the data they collected. We do however have that collected from two secondary schools, one as a part of the pilot (reported in more detail in Porter 2011) and one as part of a follow-up (reported in Porter 2013). Although the data are more limited they illustrate some of the advantages of this hybrid approach, including:

- starting with an individually compiled list ensures the pupil considers the issue from his/her own perspective;
- each has an opportunity to participate;
- discussion stimulates pupils to reflect further;
- pupils can clarify the purpose and expectations of the activity;
- it provides a sense of priority among ideas;
- the format also aids the teacher by:
  - having a clear structure for managing discussion;
  - record keeping is built into the activity.

These methods were used during the pilot work with two groups of 15 year 7 pupils withdrawn from class at a time when subjects were taught in sets. The first group was described to the research team as a 'bottom set' in which the majority of children experienced difficulty in reading. The second group was drawn from a 'middle set'. In the first group the broad question posed was: *What gets in the way of getting on in school?* Nineteen items were generated, of which 12 received votes, pupils choosing up to three items and prioritizing them by assigning 1, 2 or 3 votes. It appeared at the time that the phrasing of the question triggered responses referring to the social life of school rather than focusing on lessons and learning, although the top item, 'bunking off', is revealing of what they see as inhibiting 'getting on'. The other top responses largely refer to aspects of interaction with their peers. Notably teachers featured little in their analysis, appearing briefly in joint eighth position.

Table 5.7 Response of the first pilot focus group to *What gets in the way of getting on in school?*

Rank order of ideas		Votes
1	Bunking off	22
2	Stealing	18
3	Blackmail	13
4	Fighting	13
5	Time wasters forgetting equipment	9
6	Bullying	8
8	People who don't work as a team	5
8	People who don't concentrate	5
8	Teachers threatening people	5
10	People not participating	4
11.5	Name calling	3
11.5	Disturbing classes	3

Other items named but not receiving any votes: Physical attacking, Silly people, Trouble makers, Arguing, Noisy people, People not listening, People threaten teachers.

Because of the possibility that the phrasing of the question had inadvertently predisposed the group to highlight social aspects, the question was changed for the second group into a more neutral question: *What do you find difficult in school?*

With this group the responses were more oriented to school work and in particular more concerned with teachers and teaching, although bullying

Table 5.8 Response of the second pilot focus group to *What do you find difficult in school?*

Rank order of ideas		Votes
1	Teachers not being fair	32
2	Teachers not listening	26
3	Bullying	16
4	Teachers pick on you	16
5.5	Long lessons	11
5.5	Getting the blame unfairly	11
7.5	Friends talking and distracting	9
7.5	People who are annoying	9
9	Talking behind backs	8
10	Atmosphere	7
11	Being taught by teachers who aren't subject specialists	6
12	Lessons on the board – copying	4
13.5	Touching girls	3
13.5	Punishments	3
16	The space we work in e.g. small classrooms are claustrophobic	2
16	People turning off computers	2
16	Firewall blocking things	2

Other items: Fighting, Throwing equipment, Abusive language, Computers (arguments caused over wrong use)

featured more highly than in the previous group. Both friends and other people were equally rated as sources of interference.

In order to test further whether these differences between the two groups were a function of the question or reflected important differences between the groups, the second question was put to two groups in year 9 of a boys school in a post-project study, to test out whether we had inadvertently elicited a particular train of thought. One group were pupils with SEN and disability and the other a volunteer group withdrawn from an English lesson. The voting procedure was slightly different to that carried out in the first study and differed between the groups, with the first group having two rounds and the second only one. The data in Tables 5.9 and 5.10 reflect responses at the end of the first round of voting.

The responses of these two groups provide a number of overlapping items – eight of the items are similar but there are also some interesting differences. While Group 1 struggle with too much homework, books in the bag, checking of uniforms, repetition from the teacher, Group 2 appear more success oriented so their difficulties are things that stop them doing well, e.g. being late, missing lessons, not having work at the right level. These differences are illustrated further when the priorities are examined. Group 1 are tired, there's too much work, people don't listen to you or aren't fair, whereas for Group 2 the pressure to do well is compounded by people disrupting lessons, work set at the wrong level and the whole group being punished rather than those that transgress. These concerns of the second group were highlighted by their later

Table 5.9 Follow-up pilot, items offered by Group I and the outcome of voting

Rank	Items voted for	Total number of votes
I	One-sided teachers	10
2	Exams – too much stuff in them	9
3.5	Tired	8
3.5	Teachers don't listen to you	8
5	Lots of homework on the same day	7
6.5	When the bell doesn't go on time	6
6.5	Not liking a subject	6
8	Subject you like but don't like the teacher	5
9.5	Uniform – spend time checking it	4
9.5	Distractions – something going on in school, out of the window	4
11.5	Not enough water (drinking fountains)	3
11.5	Lunch-time run out of food	3
13	Just before exams teachers go over and over everything every day	2
14.5	Overpacked bag	I
14.5	Standing up on the bus for half an hour	I
Other items	No additional items – all those offered were voted for	

Table 5.10 Follow-up pilot, items offered by Group 2 and the outcome of voting

Rank	Item as offered	Votes
1.5	Missing out on exams due to other activities	6
1.5	Not having work set at the correct level	6
3.5	Exams – pressure to do well	5
3.5	Groups punished rather than individuals	5
5.5	People disrupting	4
5.5	Dealing with teachers you don't get on with	4
9	Being tired at school	3
9	Forgetting books and appointments	3
9	Being hungry or thirsty at school	3
9	Being uninterested in topic or lesson	3
9	Water fountains being at opposite ends of the school	3
13	Poor facilities	2
13	Having teachers who don't properly explain what they want you to do	2
13	Being late for school and lessons	2
15	Others leaving litter in the yard and we get punished	1
Other items	No additional items – all those offered were voted for	

discussion of how to remove these barriers, namely in their view by teachers being better trained to manage classes and to differentiate their teaching. The analysis of these data also extended to what pupils had added in their individual lists and this clearly revealed the tensions in the second group to do well. It also revealed however that not all items will be shared in the group setting, including items such as the following:

> Being ill for a long time and not know what is going on and having to catch up.

This is a reminder that a group setting can limit the expression of views that are felt not to be shared by the group. This brings us to examine the final set of data from the online questionnaire, a method that allows the responder to remain anonymous.

Online questionnaire

The largest group of pupils completed the online questionnaire with 25 schools offering this to pupils, including 16 primary schools (mainly used with year 4), eight secondary schools and one special school, the latter only having seven pupils complete the questionnaire. Due to the limitations of these data, the seven pupils are excluded from the following summary. In total 1,617 mainstream pupils completed the online questionnaire of whom 354 said they had a difficulty or disability, constituting some 23 per cent of the primary school returns and 21 per cent of the secondary, a notably higher percentage than the returns of parents. In part this could reflect differences between schools in the groups selected to complete the online questionnaire. Primary school samples for example offered it to between 19 and 165 children with an average of 38 pupils completing the questionnaire. The percentage of children ticking the disability or difficulty box varied between 7 per cent and 51 per cent. A similar variation can be seen between secondary schools, where the sample varied between 8 and 194 (with a mean of 105) and the percentage of disabled children between 13 per cent and 26 per cent. The larger variation in primary settings may be a factor of the larger number of schools from areas of deprivation or they could reflect younger children's uncertainty around issues of disability and difficulty. With these caveats in mind, the tables present data for disabled children with data from their peers presented alongside (in brackets). As with all questionnaires, numbers of respondents vary slightly between questions, with open questions more likely to be skipped.

Different times and places

The questionnaire begins by asking pupils to rate how they generally feel at different times and places. The ratings by children of how they felt in primary school reveals very little difference between the children who indicated they had a disability or difficulty and those who did not. Perhaps the largest difficulty lay in the likelihood of children completing the ratings with almost all disabled children indicating how they felt at different times and places. For the vast majority of children life at school is OK or better. What makes them feel especially good are school trips and, on a daily basis, break times.

Table 5.11 Online questionnaire: how disabled (and non-disabled) primary children feel at different times and places. N=180 (Non-disabled N=597)

How do you feel at different times and places?	Very good/ good	OK	Not OK	Very bad/ bad	Blank
During lessons	52%	33%	1%	1%	1%
	(53%)	(30%)	(3%)	(4%)	(11%)
During break	77 %	12%	<1	1%	0%
	(71%)	(13%)	(3%)	(1%)	(12%)
At lunch time	68%	19%	<1	1%	<1
	(67%)	(15%)	(3%)	(2%)	(12%)
Outside moving between buildings	49%	33%	1%	1%	3 %
	(48%)	(27%)	(5%)	(3%)	(17%)
During special events (like school concerts, charity days)	76%	13%	1%	1%	<1
	(65%)	(17%)	(3%)	(3%)	(12%)
On school visits and trips	91%	6%	<1	<1	1%
	(81%)	(5%)	(<1)	(1%)	(12%)

Table 5.12 Online questionnaire: how disabled (and non-disabled) secondary school children feel at different times and places. N=174 (Non-disabled N=666)

How do you feel at different times and places?	Very good/ good	OK	Not OK	Very bad/ bad	Blank
During lessons	44 %	41%	7%	6%	1%
	(43 %)	(47 %)	(3%)	(3%)	(4%)
During break	79%	17%	2%	2%	0
	(81%)	(12%)	(2%)	(<1)	(4%)
At lunch time	79%	15%	4%	2%	<1
	(79%)	(13%)	(4%)	(<1)	(4%)
Outside moving between buildings	47%	40%	8%	5%	<1
	(47%)	(42%)	(5%)	(2%)	(4)
During special events (like school concerts, charity days)	66%	22%	3%	9%	<1
	(68%)	(21%)	(4%)	(4%)	(4%)
On school visits and trips	82%	13%	<1	2%	3%
	(85%)	(8%)	(2%)	(1%)	(4%)

Turning to the secondary school pupils, again there are many similarities in the ratings of the two groups with the disabled group highly likely to complete this aspect of the form. The majority feel OK or better across the school day and feel best out of lesson time, with break and lunch time being when the majority feel good or very good and school trips providing a welcome activity. Around one in eight disabled children don't feel OK during special events or in moving around school, and given that the latter is a regular part of school life indicates the importance of this being addressed. Notably a small minority of disabled children don't feel good during lunch (6 per cent) and break time (4 per cent). These three areas of school life (break, lunch and moving around the school) all involve unstructured interactions with other pupils, ones that generally are not overseen by adults.

Following this series of rating questions there was an open question inviting children to write about what helped at particular times or places and what made things more difficult. In total 73 per cent of primary aged children who ticked the disability question provided responses, as did 80 per cent of secondary. Answers to these questions revealed the social aspects of life in school, as children mentioned people much more frequently than other aspects.

In particular what is notable is that disabled pupils turned to their friends for help and support in both primary and secondary schools. While staff featured in almost a quarter of responses of primary pupils, this fell to less than one in eight in the secondary school responses. In secondary schools peers in general were as likely to be a source of help as school staff. Families featured much less in both age groups. Pupils in general were not specific about the kind of help they provided but rather gave the impression that it was being there for them that was important. In contrast relatively few pupils cited particular lessons as being a help (8 per cent in primary and 12 per cent in secondary) and were

Table 5.13 Online questionnaire: disabled children's views of supports

What helps at different times and places	Primary N=132	Secondary N=139
Friends	34%	40%
School staff	24%	13%
Peers	8%	12%
Family	5%	4%

more likely to refer to other activities (19 per cent primary and secondary) with the younger group writing about enjoying trips out and activities such as swimming or, for both groups, the importance of break and lunch times. A smaller number of children wrote about aspects of the environment that were helpful (5 per cent primary and 17 per cent secondary). Particular aspects related to noise, to feeling safe and in secondary schools being able to move around crowded spaces. In many ways these responses pre-empted their responses to what they found difficult in school. Here it was the behaviour of peers that was particularly challenging for both primary and secondary school pupils. Pupils described the range of behaviour from bullying, name-calling, pushing, through teasing and being generally unkind. Peers also made life difficult through annoying behaviour, distracting pupils and being generally disturbing. Teachers also featured in the responses of secondary school pupils where they were described as not giving sufficient explanation, ignoring the child when their hand was up, not listening, shouting, being very strict.

Children also made some reference to specific lessons being difficult although this was more likely in primary schools where 9 per cent of responding children wrote about maths being hard and 7 per cent wrote about aspects of literacy. However 8 per cent of the responding pupils also wrote generically about hard work. Rather than listing particular subjects, pupils in the secondary schools wrote about lessons being boring, hard, unclear or irrelevant rather than refer to difficulty with the content. For a minority of children – 2 per cent in primary and 3 per cent in secondary – it was lunch and break times that were difficult. Children were more likely at secondary level to write about aspects of the environment (9 per cent primary, 20 per cent secondary). In primary school the main concern expressed was noise and seating arrangements but in secondary school children wrote about struggling with crowded areas, about queues, negotiating stairs and corridors and getting lost. Nine per cent of the

Table 5.14 Online questionnaire: disabled children's views on barriers

What makes things more difficult?	Primary N=124	Secondary N=136
Friends	5%	4%
School staff	4%	19%
Peers	30%	32%
Family	<1%	3%

responding pupils in secondary schools also expressed emotions of feeling under pressure, or stressed, feeling insecure and unsafe, awkward and uncomfortable. Only 2 per cent of pupils in primary school wrote about their emotions, feeling angry, lonely and sad.

For broader data on the whole sample we can turn to a closed question that asked pupils how often they found particular activities difficult. Looking at the tables below, over 40 per cent of disabled children in primary schools found it difficult to learn in class at least some of the time, get on with their peers, join in activities inside and outside of school. In around 10 per cent of cases this difficulty was experienced all the time. A slightly lower percentage found it difficult to get on with the adults in school. This is also true for 20–30 per cent of non-disabled pupils, although fewer, 5 per cent or less, have this experience all the time.

In secondary schools the percentages are overall slightly lower, although 43 per cent of disabled pupils experience difficulty in learning and around 30 per cent have difficulty getting on with their classmates, with teachers and joining in activities in school. However it is also clear that this is also true for a number of their peers, with a similar proportion finding it difficult to get on with their teachers and other adults in the school. Life however is generally better for their peers outside school. Whereas 24 per cent of the disabled children find it difficult to do the things they want, this is true for only 15 per cent of their peers.

If I had a magic wand

Finally turning to the last open question, *If you had a magic wand, what is the one thing you would like to change about school?*, we gain additional insights (see Table 5.17). Despite appearing towards the end of the questionnaire, 78 per cent of

Table 5.15 Online questionnaire: what disabled (and non-disabled) children in primary schools find difficult. N=180 (Non-disabled N=597)

Do you find it difficult …	Never	No not really	Yes some of the time	Yes all the time	Blank
To get on with your classmates?	22% (34%)	31% (33%)	32% (25%)	9% (5%)	6% (3%)
To learn in class?	17% (28%)	27% (36%)	40% (32%)	13% (3%)	3% (2%)
To get on with teachers and/or other people who work in the school?	33% (47%)	31% (31%)	21% (15%)	11% (4%)	4% (2%)
To join in with school activities?	22% (35%)	30% (38%)	35% (22%)	11% (5%)	2% (1%)
And what about life outside school? Do you find it difficult to do the things you want to do?	32% (34%)	23% (36%)	28% (20%)	14% (5%)	3% (5%)

Table 5.16 Online questionnaire: what disabled (and non-disabled) children in secondary
schools find difficult. N=174 (Non-disabled children N=587)

Do you find it difficult ...	Never	No not really	Yes some of the time	Yes all the time	Blank
To get on with your classmates?	31%	40%	24%	4%	<1
	(30%)	(49%)	(18%)	(2%)	(1%)
To learn in class?	11%	45%	36%	7%	<1
	(15%)	(56%)	(25%)	(3%)	(1%)
To get on with teachers and/or other people who work in the school?	25%	41%	28%	5%	<1
	(18%)	(49%)	(29%)	(3%)	(1%)
To join in with school activities?	20%	47%	25%	6%	3%
	(27%)	(51%)	(17%)	(4%)	(<1)
And what about life outside school? Do you find it difficult to do the things you want to do?	30%	43%	20%	4%	4%
	(39%)	(44%)	(11%)	(4%)	(2%)

children who stated they had a disability or difficulty and 77 per cent of the rest of the sample responded with some interesting differences between primary and secondary pupil responses. Taking the disabled group first, the primary aged children were more likely to write about lessons and activities (23 per cent), particularly that they were too hard, they wanted them to be easier with more opportunities for play. They also wrote about school rules and structures (22 per cent). They would particularly like to increase the length of break and lunch times. Disabled pupils at secondary school would use their magic wand to change their social relationships (35 per cent), with equal mention being made of the behaviour of other children as of the behaviour of staff. The former they wanted to be kinder, less nasty, the latter fairer, more helpful, less strict.

Just under 10 per cent of disabled primary and secondary school pupils said they would change the behaviour of bullies.

My best friend to stop being bullied.

People struggling with bullying.

I would not get called names and laughed at and teased.

Secondary school pupils (29 per cent) also wrote about changing lessons and activities, the former should be more interesting and fun, with more opportunities for sport, art and practical work, less English and maths. There were also a high number of comments relating to school rules and practices (30 per cent). They wanted less (or no) homework, no uniforms. As with the younger group, there was too short a time allocated to lunch and break. Overall some 17 per cent of this disabled group also made comments about changing aspects of the physical environment or resources. Both primary and secondary school children wrote about aspects of size and decor of their classroom/school, and the secondary group also wrote about cleanliness. The primary school children were more likely to conjure up equipment with their magic wands, particularly for the playground.

There were also a number of individual comments relating to aspects of themselves that they would change.

> To be able to learn fast so that I can be the same as every one else in my class.

> I'd like to be more popular.

> Not having the headaches.

> I would like to have no rowles [rules] or fights and be good.

If we look briefly at the comments made by the other children, we see that there is less mention of social relationships although it is still an important element of secondary school pupil responses and with a smaller proportion mentioning bullying, although, as with both groups, comments about being picked on and teased might easily also fall within this category. Primary school pupil responses are more distributed across categories, with people being the focus as much as physical aspects of their environment. Secondary school pupils typically wrote as the disabled group had done of wanting no uniform, no

Table 5.17 Online questionnaire: what disabled (and non-disabled) pupils would change. N=276 (Non-disabled N=1,252)

Areas to change	Primary N=137	Secondary N=139	Total 78% (77%) N=276
Social relationships	20% (15%)	35% (24%)	28% (20%)
Behaviour of others	15% (11%)	24% (17%)	20% (14%)
Rules and structures	22% (12%)	30% (33%)	26% (23%)
Lessons and activities	23% (14%)	29% (26%)	26% (20%)
Self	7% (3%)	6% (1%)	7% (2%)
Environment and resources	18% (16%)	16% (9%)	17% (12%)
Generic	9% (5%)	9% (5%)	9% (5%)
Bullying	9% (3%)	9% (5%)	9% (4%)

homework and with imaginative variations of how to shorten time spent at school, from long weekends, shorter working weeks, fewer weeks in the year. Generic comments often referred to different ways in which they would close the school. Few pupils at either phase mentioned changing aspects of themselves.

> I would stop people bullying and saying horible things to people. somtimes people dont reolize how much they can hurt someone and make them feel so small and insignificant and stupid. i would stop that compleatly no mater were you go or who you are everybody gets name called ect.

It's important to look within the aggregated data to understand the experience of those who might fall within the minority but whose experiences in school are bad. For example one pupil in secondary school rated every aspect of school between not OK and bad or very bad, the only OK rating going to trips outside school. Her comment about what helps refers to '*nowt school can do*' and we learn more when she writes about what helps in lessons '*all bad cos of the kids I like ict and art cos you work on your own*'. In response to being a given a magic wand her response is simple – to change '*the people*'. Given the ratings and comments together this pupil clearly needed some additional support in developing better relationships with other children.

Of course not all children with consistently low ratings volunteered information about what would help – one primary school boy simply responded to being asked 'can you tell me …?' by writing '*no*' in every open question. Fortunately he indicated on his form that he would turn to peers and teachers for support. He elected to write his name on the form, enabling teachers and other staff to find an opportunity to elicit more information from him about what the barriers and supports were. These examples illustrate the importance of schools looking within the data to understand both group and individual experiences.

Discussion

Previous studies eliciting the views of disabled young people have largely been small scale and have often taken a specific impairment focus. In many ways therefore the data from this project provides us with a unique opportunity to look at a wide-ranging group of young people from over 40 schools and examine whether there are any reoccurring themes, any shared meaning to attach to the nature of barriers and supports for disabled children. However in doing so there are a number of caveats. The methods and activities were designed for staff to use flexibly and to draw conclusions that related to their own particular context. Details of how they chose participants are not always clear and nor often are the particular age groups, so we can only examine phase related differences and these may obscure changes in views across year groups. Children self-identify as disabled (as indeed do adults) and in recognition of literature that indicates that difficulty rather than disability may be a better term we identify our disabled population accordingly. This is a strength of the data and again enables us to include children who, because they don't have a special educational need, are easily overlooked. Data from pupils in special schools are more limited, with the exception of the school for children with social, emotional and behavioural difficulties (SEBD), most special schools only used the materials with a small number of children. Given these parameters a short review of the findings suggests there are some strong messages that emerge from the data.

Overview of findings

'Good and bad things about school' was typically used with the youngest children and revealed their difficulty in commenting about people, compared with activities or places. Canteens and toilets were locations of difficulty and there was a growing awareness of feeling different – PE could be a tricky time. The symbol questionnaire data from special school pupils revealed that assembly and circle time were particularly disliked, a sentiment shared by the primary school children. Children in both settings wanted help in making friends. This aspect, together with playing with others, was seen to be almost as difficult as doing their work. Further data on special school pupils were gained using point to point methods with primary aged special school pupils with SEBD. This revealed that despite the focus on specific events children often found moments of change and times of unpredictability particularly difficult. Pupils appeared more likely than other groups to comment on their own behaviour, in the context of interactions with others.

Data from the online questionnaire suggested that in both primary and secondary schools there were strong similarities between the children who ticked the difficulties/disability question and the rest of the cohort. Disabled children felt generally OK in school, and break times, unsurprisingly, are when they feel best. The hardest times appear to be outside, moving around the buildings, and lessons, but still the majority generally feel OK or better. Generally disabled pupils feel better in primary schools than secondary where some 12–15 per cent rate their experiences as not OK, bad or very bad, during lessons, outside moving around and at special events. These bad feelings are less likely to be shared by their non-disabled peers. Friends in both settings were the prime sources of support, but this is especially true of disabled pupils in secondary schools. In primary school disabled children also look to staff for help but this is not true of the majority of secondary school pupils.

Noise, feeling safe and moving around crowded spaces were referred to in the open questions as areas of difficulty for disabled pupils. In secondary schools what they find difficult is the behaviour of peers, pushing, teasing, name-calling and disrupting lessons. They also find teachers' behaviour difficult and unhelpful. Generally there were issues about lessons being too hard, not fun and in secondary schools this was compounded by the pressure to do well. The magic wand question revealed priorities in what pupils would change. Whereas disabled children in primary schools wrote about lessons and activities and increasing free time and the purchase of new (play) equipment, secondary school pupils would change aspects of their social relationships. Almost one in ten children in both settings would use their magic wand against bullies.

The focus group data revealed differences between groups in their judgements concerning the behaviour of others. On the one hand pupils could find the behaviour of others challenging because it hurt them (or their property) in some way. On the other hand, for others, it was the impact of the behaviour on their own learning, stopping them concentrating or leading to the class being punished. The barriers were therefore ones that impacted on their attainment.

It appears that it is the social aspects of schooling that particularly impinge on children, and that these often (but not always) concern the informal aspects of school life. These involve the times and spaces/places of the school that make children feel best but that can also be most troubling. Even though the youngest children found it difficult to talk about others they identified places that called on their use of social skills (namely canteens and toilets). Their responses however also revealed that they found activities that largely involved sitting and listening (such as assemblies and circle time) problematic, and in contrast wanted more time to play. They wanted help not only with work but with making friends. It is perhaps unsurprising that with age these views crystallize. Secondary schools pose additional demands with an increase in workload, including homework, and possibly longer hours, placing greater academic pressure on young people. At the same time there is a need to be more self-reliant in finding one's way around a larger environment, moving between lessons and teachers and groups, placing a demand for greater interpersonal skills at a time when they feel there is a lower level of support (Hughes et al. 2013; Maras and Aveling 2006; Powell et al. 2006). Given these changes one would expect to see differences in their views with age.

In secondary school the data on barriers to participation focus on relationships, interactions with peers and those with teachers. Whereas in primary school pupils look to both friends and teachers for support, it is the former that are key to survival – a buffer in the face of adversity. Our data are consistent with those of other studies that reveal the role of friends in providing support and motivation as well as opportunities to talk about one's feelings – including studies of boys (Irwin 2013). 'Hanging out with mates' provides a reason for going to school (Irwin 2013). Support is particularly needed to offset negative interactions from others. Given special powers many would 'zap' bullies. There is compelling evidence across a range of studies, both national and international, that disabled children are more likely to be bullied. Naylor et al. (2012) state that bullying is three times more likely amongst 13–14 year olds, Blake et al. (2012) estimate that in the United States between a quarter and a third of disabled young people experience bullying, while Connors and Stalker (2002) estimate almost half. Evangelou *et al.* (2008) report on a study of transitions and an analysis of successful transitions. Importantly for our study they indicated that children with SEN were much more likely to be bullied – some 37 per cent, compared with 25 per cent of other children, who 'had problems with bullying'. Looking across their sample there was a clear relationship between making new friends, raised self-esteem and successful transitions from primary to secondary schools.

Other studies suggest that some disabled groups are more likely than others to experience bullying. Naylor *et al.* (2012) and Blake *et al.* (2012) both indicate a higher incidence for children on the autistic spectrum (and in the case of the Naylor study also children with speech and language difficulties and those with learning difficulties). Ytterhus (2012), in a longitudinal study of Norwegian children, exposes the hidden school curriculum with informal rules of social interaction operating, which over time become increasingly nuanced. The toughest time appeared to be ages 10–14 with the introduction of mandating rules and establishment of sub-groups that created identities. Children that did not understand the nuances were likely to be marginalized. This may explain the ways in which some groups of disabled young people become the target of bullies. Pellegrini (2002) argues that bullying increases as a function of striving for status amongst one's peers and the development of affiliations and cliques. The relationship between school size is unclear although Pellegrini argues that there is less bullying in small co-operative schools and that in part this is because of the consistency of contact between individuals – the antithesis of the experience of some young people in secondary schools.

Briefly one might contrast pupil views with that of parents who focus on the presence of adults to support their child, not recognizing that this can serve as both a help and a hindrance (Rutherford 2011). In contrast the role of friends is more rarely mentioned by parents, and when it does occur they often refer to family friends, support for the whole family, rather than their child's peer group. Lewis *et al.* (2006) also comment on differences in parent and child views with parents wanting a clear system of support and pupils favouring flexibility with opportunities for choice. There are other similarities to our data in this Disability Rights commissioned work, as the children's views also highlight the importance of friends and the ways in which these may be restricted out of school. They also write about difficulties experienced in unstructured activities such as break and lunch time and the greater occurrences of bullying. One of the messages of their report is the importance of key staff that smooth the passage of access and arrangements, an issue to return to later in the book. Communicating a positive ethos is not enough, staff play an important role in enabling peers to get to know and understand a disabled child whose impairment impacts on their interactions with peers (Naraian 2011). There are also more easily grasped implications for teachers in considering seating arrangements, and enabling pupils to work collaboratively and get along with others.

We were interested that while pupils did mention the environment in relation to difficulties, these were very likely to be in relation to noise and safety, both important issues in relation to reducing stress and anxiety within school. The environment also has implications for interactions. When spaces are crowded and it is difficult to hear others, there is increased potential for communications to break down, and more physical types of communication to be used. Actions speak louder than words, particularly when the acoustics are poor. Children also demonstrated the importance of the environment when it came to using their magic wand. A brighter, lighter, more colourful environment would provide a better venue for daily attendance. Younger children in particular focused on the importance of the playground, a space that can promote interaction or provide a highly inaccessible space. As Yantzi et al. (2010) conclude, 'The sense of belonging or not belonging is shaped by practices, policies, constructions, assumptions, values and priorities that influence how spaces are designed and organised and how spaces function' (pp. 66–67). Given the opportunity, children had many ideas that would improve the functioning of their school environment.

There was resonance between our findings and that of other large-scale mainstream studies. Flutter and Rudduck (2004) for example write about the importance pupils attribute to break times and the opportunity for unstructured activities when they can have fun, be active and socialize, but they were also a time with potential for negative interaction. Their analysis suggested that pupils can find these unstructured times boring with too little to do. Like pupils in our sample they cite suggestions for restructuring the school day – starting earlier and finishing earlier. (Such suggestions were contradicted in our study by the desire of some pupils to start later.) Pupils spoke about the challenge of missing school – of having to catch up – sentiments expressed by some of our disabled sample, and Flutter and Rudduck suggest that this is an increasing concern as they approach year 11. Notably they state that 'few teachers would disagree that, for pupils, the social dimensions of classroom life often take precedence over the academic' (p. 102). As they observe for many primary aged pupils, there may be relatively little contact with the teacher and most of the time spent working with other pupils. It is perhaps hardly surprising then that these relationships become the source of support when pupils don't understand the task that has been set, and that this 'sets the stage' for the importance of peers at secondary school. Additionally there is an important affective dimension, providing confidence and self-esteem that goes beyond pupils' achievements and learning. Pedder and McIntyre (2006) write about the importance of social capital, having mutually respectful and trusting relationships, with both teachers and peers, that support the achievement of shared goals. It is the existence of this trust that supports the communication of views and the receptivity of teachers to respond to pupil views. Pedder and McIntyre (2006) distinguish between high- and low-achieving pupils. The latter experience more difficulty articulating their views, with general statements about preferring practical and fun activities. High-achieving pupils are more detailed and precise, not only in relation to how they learn but also how others learn best. Disabled pupils may of course fall within either group. An alternative analysis is to consider the extent to which children share the same learning agenda as teachers and how this in turn impacts on teachers' readiness to listen to pupils' views. Pedder and McIntyre illustrate the extent to which different teachers internalize the importance of being receptive and trusting of pupil ideas, leading some teachers to view it as a single occasion exercise and others to embed it within their classroom practice. One implication from our research is that the common agenda of learning needs to extend to incorporate the important area of peer relationships, to embody for example collaborative learning, reducing the emphasis on individual competition in attainment.

Finally we turn to the implications of the data for the methods for eliciting pupil views. Much has already been written, indeed more than on the content of children's views themselves, so the following are specific to the discoveries made while analysing and reflecting on the data. It was pleasing that the methods had largely not pre-empted the views of children. The use of words of time and place and people were sufficiently broad to be interpreted by pupils without a fixed agenda that all adults were interested in was the barriers and supports to learning. There was therefore opportunity to investigate what school life meant for children, and to find that the social life can be more important than the academic. In suggesting that schools collect data from all children, not just those who were known to be disabled, there was opportunity to uncover the continuum of aspects that children struggled with as well as what they found helpful.

Not all methods provided opportunities for anonymity or for silence. We relied on schools to follow the guidance of being sensitive to pupil responses and to respect their wishes not to take part. The online questionnaire, the method that provided data from the greatest number of children, had many advantages in this respect. Children could opt to leave questions blank and although we provided space towards the end for them to indicate whether they would like to speak to someone about the issues raised and invited them to indicate who this might be, it was only at this point that we offered them the possibility of writing their name. It was therefore only requested if they wanted support provided. Clearly as we have seen from some of the responses some children felt that nothing could be done. In some cases schools were frustrated by the anonymity provided by the questionnaire but it respected the right of pupils to silence (Lewis 2004) and the freedom to give views that might be seen as subversive or ones that they would not want to freely share with others. In doing so we allowed the views of the individual to be voiced. While not all schools used the online method, research has suggested that pupils write more (Hill 2006) and that it is less likely to present as a school task. It also has the advantage for schools in providing an easily accessible report on which to base their decisions for introducing change.

The methods used were not definitive by any means. We could also have provided guidance on using diamond ranking (Thomas and O'Kane 1998), self-reports to video, aka Big Brother, photographic or video trails. However schools readily demonstrated their creativity in developing methods to engage children, but also in many cases electing to use more straightforward structured methods. Particular methods could have changes made, the use of the term 'sometimes' on the symbol questionnaire (in places to replace uncertain) and the insertion of 'working with others'. On the online questionnaire, an examination of the extent to which the second open question provided additional information. These are small adjustments and it should be emphasized that the tools were designed as the first stage in establishing a dialogue with pupils with the important message provided here that it is not simply a case of asking pupils about learning and subject choices. The more tricky issues of social relationships need grasping and these will require changes in staff behaviour as much as pupil and peer interaction. While government policy is focussed on subject teaching, it is the hidden curriculum that prepares and supports disabled pupils in their participation in school life and beyond.

Chapter 6

Using disability data in schools

Introduction

Parent and pupil data provided important information about the barriers encountered and what support the children found useful. They provided vital insights into the subjective experience of disability, drawing attention to the ways in which this varies with the context and to differences in the perspectives of parents and children. Children in particular drew attention to the informal aspects of schooling, the unstructured times during the day where interactions with others can lead to some disabled children finding school a bad or very bad experience. While younger children will consider the barriers in terms of lessons and activities, for older pupils it is interaction with others, staff and pupils, that they can find difficult. This may pass under the radar of staff whose attention may be directed largely to the classroom and achievement and may not be fully aware of the strong relation between learning, relationships and wellbeing, especially where the educational climate privileges attainment and position in league tables. While parents also seem to focus on adult support for their child, which they express in relation to teaching assistant support and individual learning, their comments with respect to attitudes and understanding of staff suggest they are also concerned about the wellbeing of their child. Unlike pupils, however, there is little mention of the child's peer group or more importantly their friends. Relationships feature strongly in how connected a pupil is to their school (McLaughlin and Clarke 2010) and arguably these frame how adjustments are received and whether they contribute to supporting the child. Without this knowledge schools are limited in the effectiveness of the responses they make. The quality and completeness of this information is therefore vital.

The purpose of the project was to devise user-friendly tools so that schools could collect their own information and respond accordingly. The whole premise on which the project is based would however be impeded if the methods proved unusable to schools, if schools did not learn anything from the data and if they did not make use of the data. This chapter sets out to explore these issues. The chapter will draw on interview data with parents, professionals in schools and local authorities together with observations of children in class. It will explore data that indicated discrepancies between that provided by parents and the views within an organization. It will illustrate the process that schools used to optimize their data collection and provide case study examples of how they used the outcomes to inform their policies and practices. Most of the data come from phase 2 of the project which directly addressed issues of the use and usability of the data, including measures of reliability in schools reporting on the data. However, where relevant and available, data from phase 1 are also presented.

Do the data contribute new knowledge for schools?

It is important to explore the extent to which the parental questionnaire revealed new information for schools, whether or not the returns identify students with disabilities not previously known to the school, and whether it provided additional information about children already known to have a health condition or impairment. A third aspect relates to whether schools were able to use this information to make changes, either at the level of the individual child or more widely with respect to policies and practices for the whole school. We anticipated that schools would learn new information as in the first phase of the project researchers made visits to eight mainstream schools and four special schools and in each case we found when interviewing staff that the data had revealed information about pupils which was unknown to the school.

In the second phase of the study all schools were asked to report back to us and, overall, about one-third of schools recorded unanticipated findings from the parental questionnaire ('surprises'). The numbers of surprises were distributed fairly evenly across the three types of school: four out of 14 secondary schools reported surprises; eight of the 23 primary schools; and three of the eight special schools. Most of the surprises related to students who were identified as disabled by parents but whose difficulties were not recorded in this way by schools; and these difficulties tended to be health related (e.g. difficulties associated with asthma). The exception was in special schools, where two of the three 'surprises' related to parents' judgements that their child's difficulties did not meet 'disability' criteria, which was in contrast to the schools' views; furthermore in one secondary school a number of pupils judged as disabled by the school were not viewed as such by parents. Unsurprisingly, the number of 'surprises' per school was relatively low – most schools that reported 'surprises' identified one or two students in this category. However, one secondary school reported a comparatively high number (12) of such cases: six students identified by parents who were not listed by the school as disabled (but two were known to the school nurse); and, conversely, six students identified as disabled by the school who were not rated as such by parents.

In order to understand differences between school and parent information and how schools could be surprised by parent data we carried out some observations of children in class. This took place in 15 primary schools, 14 secondary schools and eight special schools, with a total of 42 children, just under a third, where the parental responses had surprised the school. In this way we aimed to examine the validity of the data for all children. Researchers carried out a short narrative observation over a 40-minute period, noting in particular the level of participation and engagement of the pupil, any barriers and supports to learning and any areas of need that were notable during the session. We used a scale, adapted from that of Laevers *et al.* (2002) to monitor involvement and engagement ranging from level 1 (shows little or no involvement or activity) to level 5 (shows high and sustained involvement) during the observed lessons. Although this was an approximate measure it served to indicate how well engaged in the lesson the pupil was and therefore whether or not schools might have concerns because the level of involvement was very low or whether they would be assured by high levels of participation.

Case studies where the response to the parental questionnaire surprised the school

Surprise children who did not participate fully in class

Of the 13 surprise children, there were five children whose class participation could be judged to be problematic. They were scored as 1 or 2 on a five-point scale, that is they were not participating in an activity, showing little awareness of what was going on in the classroom, little receptivity to the learning opportunities on offer or they showed small fleeting moments of involvement or participation. Of these five there were four cases where the school was surprised that the parents did not report the same order of difficulty observed in school. The case below illustrates a difference where the child experienced no substantial impact at home but did in school:

> Laura attends a mainstream secondary school. She did not speak in school but did at home. The staff were aware of Laura's difficulties and had been specifically asked not to put pressure on her to speak. In the classroom she did not engage with the primary task, which was a maths test, and she spent much of her time looking around the room in a distracted and 'dreamy' fashion. Her teacher said that she was often like this in class. Her parents answered that her condition was long-standing on the questionnaire although they did not consider that it had an impact on her daily life. They did feel that she experienced difficulty interacting with classmates and with speaking and understanding others. The young person had been seen by a hypnotist and a doctor.

The opposite case is illustrated where the school was surprised and had not recognized the barriers to progress. The child was a boy who had spina bifida which was unknown to staff in the school. As we can see from the details below parents had important information to share with them:

> On the questionnaire Michael's parents indicated that his condition was long-standing and that it frequently gave rise to difficulties in participating in activities outside the classroom in school and outside the home.
>
>> He finds it hard to walk effectively. He has numb feet and ankles and constant foot ulcers and trauma to his feet. His poor circulation causes slow healing.
>
> They stated that he had no support in school and that he is unable to do contact sports such as rugby, football or running because of the risk of trauma to his feet and ankles and his extremely delicate spine. They wrote that he has to stand or sit and watch, and isn't given alternative activities. The young person had been seen by a doctor, a paediatrician, a neurosurgeon and a physiotherapist.
>
> When observed in class it appeared that his participation was problematic. He was intermittently engaged in the classroom tasks and appeared to have difficulty in discerning exactly what it was he was supposed to be doing. His teacher suggested that he was easily distracted and that he could be frustrated and behave in an erratic manner. He has a record of poor attendance.
>
> The school were aware that he was experiencing difficulties but not all staff were aware of the exact cause. The school's 'Specific Medical Difficulties' sheet has now been updated by the Matron and re-published to staff.

Surprise children who were observed to participate in class

Observations on the remaining eight surprise children suggested that they were engaged in class activities. Seven of the eight showed good levels of involvement, the activity appeared to have meaning for them and they were engaged, sometimes intensely so. The eighth child showed more or less sustained activity (although it lacked intensity). These then were children who, at least on casual observation, would not be a cause for concern to the school. Interestingly this included cases where the condition had no impact at home, only at school, and indeed on short observation it appeared not to be the cause of problems at school, i.e. the school had successfully made the necessary adjustments. However there were also two cases where schools would have benefitted from more information as both led to absences at school. This included a child for whom the impact of asthma caused school attendance difficulties, and another whose migraine attacks also caused school absence. Schools therefore were unaware because when the impact was experienced they did not attend school.

Case studies where the response to the parental questionnaire had not surprised the school

The researchers also made observations of 29 children whose parents' reports on the questionnaire did not surprise the school. Of these, five were children whose class participation was judged to be problematic (scored as 1 or 2 the five-point scale). All of these were cases where very visible conditions were reported, e.g. ADHD, SLD/PMLD, ADD and ASD, one in special school and the others in primary schools. The majority of pupils were however showing good levels of participation in the learning opportunities offered to them.

Overall the data suggest that schools are aware of difficulties that give rise to problems with participation in class. However the parental questionnaire surfaced experienced difficulties that remain invisible to the school and have hitherto been unreported. They also revealed cases where there was no difficulty experienced outside the school. The observations therefore reinforced the importance of schools understanding the contextual nature of disability, recognizing that the experience of a health condition or impairment can vary substantially across settings and that they can only gain a full picture through learning about this from the parent and child.

How can schools use the data?

In phase 2 of the project we asked schools directly how they planned to use the data. Responses from 20 schools (out of 45) indicated that a range of benefits emerged from conducting the survey. Interestingly, this number included four of the seven special schools (where it might be anticipated that staff would be knowledgeable about the range and impacts of children's difficulties), one of whom commented, 'We get a lot of information from Statements … but this is much more detailed than current SIMS data'. A staff member of a second special school said: 'It is an interesting exercise to get people to think more deeply about the DDA definition of disability.'

Similar statements were made by other schools:

> We haven't ever collected specific data in such depth for disability and similarly a secondary school stated that it provided 'more detailed knowledge'.
>
> (Head of a primary school in Somerset)

> We will improve our data collection as a result of this survey ... [because it] adds to 'whole picture' knowledge.
>
> (High school head)

Other comments about positive benefits included the following topics:

- Opportunities (provided by the questionnaire) for parents to voice their views/concerns about their child's difficulties.
- The process provides more detailed information for the school, e.g. about impact, and 'about *what* the disability is'.
- Current documentation relies on information gained from the primary transfer process and from parents' evenings (the implication being that these sources do not provide sufficiently detailed information).
- A prompt that information about accidents or traumas needs to be included in the school's records.
- The data highlight the needs of students who have recently been admitted and/or who are mid-phase entrants.

A local authority adviser stated: 'schools thinking changed as a result of the questionnaire [parent] ... the impact question was brilliant'. It got them to 'move on from mobility and health needs'. 'It's not just a paper exercise ... [it's] about identification and conducive environments.'

Twenty schools (out of 45) indicated the action they would take as a result of the data collected from the parental questionnaire. Five schools anticipated using the data as an additional check (e.g. to ensure that the schools' current records – including medical records – are comprehensive); five schools will use the data to inform plans for targeting or monitoring support for students; and four schools planned to contact parents to follow-up issues they had mentioned. Two schools commented that this exercise would contribute to better data collection in future: 'This needs to be included in what we are already doing'; and 'We will improve our data collection as a result of this survey'. Two schools commented that the data would help identify students' difficulties, for example, 'to highlight any undiscovered issues mentioned by parents'. Other matters raised by schools included using the survey information to liaise with other professionals about health problems; to update information without targeting students suspected of having disability status; to inform pastoral/SEN planning; to contribute to the school development plan and disability scheme; to inform possible continuing professional development events; and using the information to review and update information on students' statements. A member of staff in one school considered that the data added to the 'whole picture' by increasing specific knowledge of students' difficulties, and in similar vein, another member of staff commented, 'It will help the school to improve [our] response to diverse needs'.

In 2011 we invited two schools to present how they had used the tools following our involvement in the study at an ESRC Festival of Social

Science event. The head of a first school said that the questionnaire, because of its appearance, had a surprisingly high response rate and consequently she had used it in the subsequent year. She illustrated the benefits of using the data both on strategic planning and to the benefit of individual children. It provided a way of distinguishing between the impairment they had on school entry with the impact of this and gave them insights into how it affected pupils at home, enabling them to better support parents as well as pupils in the school. The deputy head of a secondary school discussed how the research had enabled her to consider how they meet the needs of disabled pupils in the longer term. She reported how they had used the parent disability questionnaire and the flexible pupil methods to identify things that help learning and those which prevent them. As a result they have:

*   focussed as a whole school on improving the quality of teaching and learning and tackling low level disruption;
*   invested in new signage to help pupils navigate around the school;
*   liaised better with primary schools to find out in more detail what is covered in the curriculum.

Interestingly no school explicitly identified the role of the data in monitoring pupil progress.

Monitoring attainment

One of the key purposes of the Equality Act is to ensure that pupils are not being discriminated against, that they have fair and equal access to opportunities for learning. Previous studies have highlighted how disabled children are more likely to leave school with lower or no qualifications and, despite having had similar aspirations to other young people, are more likely to find themselves unemployed in their twenties (Burchardt 2005). Other studies similarly report on the ways in which disability reduces the life chances of a child or young person. There is therefore an important role for schools in ensuring that children are supported both to participate in school life and to achieve. Notably government figures for improving attainment are restricted to pupils with SEN. The Government Office for Disability Issues has provided the following statistics:

Between 2005/06 and 2010/11, the percentage of pupils at the end of Key Stage 4 achieving 5 or more GCSE or equivalent qualifications at grades A*–C has:

*   increased from 66.3 per cent to 88.9 per cent for pupils without Special Educational Needs (SEN);
*   increased from 19.8 per cent to 59.2 per cent for pupils with SEN without a statement;

- increased from 8.7 per cent to 24.9 per cent for pupils with SEN with a statement.

(http://odi.dwp.gov.uk/disability-statistics-and-research/
disability-equality-indicators.php)

This of course ignores the attainment of those disabled pupils who don't have a special educational need and it is to this group that we now turn. In the first phase of the project we matched the data from the parental questionnaire to the National Pupil Database (NPD). Full details can be found in Porter *et al.* (2008). We asked the question: *Are disabled pupils making comparable progress?* In matching the data to the NPD, the team were able to compare the performance of disabled pupils with their peers, and look at whether they met expectations, that is to say the predicted progress. At the time of writing the report data were not available for those pupils whose attainments were described as below level 1 of the National Curriculum. Data were also limited for the youngest children where only a small percentage had Foundation Stage profile data. We were however able to examine KS1 data from 812 year 4 primary school children and KS1 and 2 data from 845 year 8 secondary school pupils.

Given that schools are already making some response to pupils with special educational needs, we were particularly interested to track the progress of those children who were disabled but did not have a special educational need. We found that the KS1 pupils were doing as well as their peers across all four subjects, reading, writing, maths and science. The same was true of the attainment of year 8 pupils at KS2. We went on to examine the value added data of these year 8 pupils, that is to say we compared their attainment at KS2 against their starting point (or prior attainment) at KS1. Level 4 is taken as the expected level of achievement and 97 per cent of the disabled group (without SEN) were *expected* to perform at level 4 or above. Just over 90 per cent reached this level, with 9 per cent of the disabled group more than two points below their predicted scores, compared with 12 per cent of their non-disabled peers, suggesting that overall their progress was similar.

We went on to undertake the now controversial contextual value added analysis. This methodology calculates progress after adjustments have been made to take into account a number of factors: gender, ethnicity, first language, age, movement between schools, special educational needs, eligibility for free school meals and family circumstances. This revealed that disabled children without special educational needs generally make progress as expected but there were a group of children who were not doing as well as projected. They were largely children who were performing above level 4 and for whom schools may therefore be satisfied with their attainment and whose under-achievement may go unnoticed.

In January 2012 the government dropped the use of contextual value added in league tables, arguing that it is too complex for parents to really understand. There was also concern that it had inadvertently lowered expectations for some groups. There is also an unresolved debate about how best to measure value added with debate amongst academics on the best methodology, and strong concerns about its use to indicate school effectiveness (Dearden *et al.* 2011; Gorard 2011; Kelly and Downey 2010).

Two charts are included here that illustrate the way in which a secondary school can use value added data to look at the performance of groups (as in Figure 6.1) and of individuals, to identify those who are performing below the level expected (as in the case of Sue in Figure 6.2) and who may benefit from looking at what adjustments may be necessary.

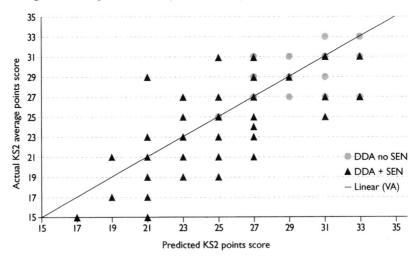

Figure 6.1 Attainment of year 8 disabled children with and without special educational needs using value added data.

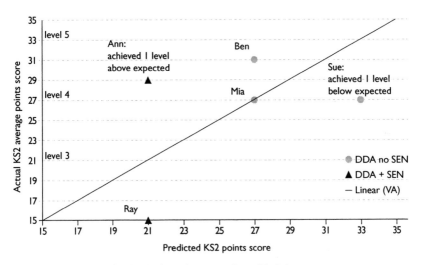

Figure 6.2 Attainment of individual pupils using value added data.

Supporting schools in collecting the data

Ensuring equitable outcomes for disabled children requires schools to have identified them together with the barriers to participation and therefore schools need to be confident that they have received relevant information from all their parents. They need therefore to have high return rates to their questionnaire. In the next section I turn to the issue of return rates and the strategies schools used to improve these.

Return rates

In many ways schools were well supported in the project. They were provided with all the materials necessary for surveying parents, including the specified number of questionnaires with a covering letter already inserted in envelopes with a return envelope together with a timeline for action. Attention already had been given to length of the parental questionnaire, and the formatting, so it was visually appealing with a clear layout, simple routing and some use of colour. Parents were given clear information about the purpose of collecting data, which concerned 'making schools better places for learning' for all children.

It was also notable from returns to the previous survey that some parents (<1 per cent) were reticent about this information being communicated to other professionals, highlighting the tensions in sharing sensitive data. Parents need to trust that the information will be used to the benefit of their child; and they need assurances that appropriate procedures will be in place to ensure confidentiality. Schools had also been briefed on these issues and identified a named person to whom the questionnaire would be returned and read and this information was shared with parents. In addition to informing parents who would have access to their information, they were also given options for indicating further confidentiality on the questionnaire form.

Schools were also given reminder letters for sending out one week later and briefed on how to maximize return rates including the benefits of preliminary notification, the importance of sending out the reminder letters with examples provided of what schools had done in the past to encourage parents to complete the questionnaires.

Most schools reported that they found the process of distributing and gathering data from parents unproblematic. Almost half the schools in the second phase (20 out of 45) opted to alert parents before sending out the questionnaire. Of these, most sent parents a briefing letter or included information about the questionnaire in a school newsletter (13 schools). Other briefing/preparation methods used across both phases included mentioning the questionnaire in a school assembly, displaying the questionnaire at a parents' evening, introducing the questionnaire in the school newsletter, inviting parents to a coffee morning, and asking a home–school link worker to liaise with key families.

The great majority of schools distributed the questionnaire to parents by sending it home with students (35 out of 45 schools in phase 2). Two schools handed the questionnaire to parents personally, and one school did both (sent it via students and handed it to parents personally). Schools went to considerable lengths to ensure a good return: 31 schools chased up parents by sending a reminder letter home with students; and other schools used a variety of creative methods to remind parents, e.g. using a text messaging system, and posting up reminders on a daily bulletin board in the playground. Schools in phase 1 also reported reminding parents in the newsletter and again in assembly, reminding children to remind parents and offering an inducement to pupils (house points) and classes with the highest number of returns.

Committed schools therefore used tried and tested methods to increase their return rates, demonstrating their awareness of the importance of this information. On the whole schools where the return rate was low were unsurprised, reporting that they usually struggled to get parents to return forms. Conversely there were some schools where the return rate surprised them and they suggested that this was due to the formal appearance of the questionnaire giving the information particular status. The overall return rate was 42 per cent, which, despite a tighter time scale, was exactly comparable with previous phases of the project (Porter *et al.* 2008). As with the previous phase secondary schools provided both the highest and lowest response rate. Notably the school with the lowest rate was recruited by being nominated by their local authority without their prior agreement, and received briefing through the post only. They therefore did not receive direct personal communication nor the opportunity to raise questions or voice concerns. This school had no time to brief parents before the questionnaires were sent out but did issue the reminder letters.

Despite being quicker and easier to complete, online responses represented less than 2 per cent of the returns for the majority of schools. Few schools (eight) judged it necessary to offer support to parents. However, one school commented that although no parents asked for help, it would have been better to have informed parents that they could contact the school's parent adviser if help with completing the questionnaire was needed.

In general the findings revealed that the lowest response rates came from schools in local authorities in the most deprived areas whereas the highest return rates came from schools with average or below average numbers of

Table 6.1 Return rates by school type in phase 2 (phase 1) of the project

Phase	Average return rates	Minimum return rate	Maximum return rate
Primary	51% (42%)	27% (10%)	71% (78%)
Secondary	35% (39%)	5% (14%)	83% (80%)
Special	49% (46%)	31% (29%)	75% (78%)

pupils on free school meals (FSM). However there were schools with above average levels of FSM whose return rates exceeded the average – and of course the converse, schools with low return rates despite having a relatively privileged catchment area. One implication is for schools to consider whether a self-completed questionnaire is the best mode for collecting these data.

Reliability in the use of the data

An important element of reporting on disability is to facilitate consistent interpretation of the returns across schools. To this end schools were provided with guidance on how to identify pupils that meet the legal criteria by considering responses to combinations of questions. They were invited to use this sifting guide to complete a brief online census form entering only disabled children. Thirty-six schools completed the online census form and also returned their questionnaires (the remainder either returned the forms without entering them on the census or completed the census but did not return the forms).

The schools identified a total of 318 pupils, with 93 per cent of the children also identified by the research team, as meeting the criteria. However schools included an additional 110 children, under a third of whom reported any impact, suggesting that schools had not taken this into account in identifying who met the criteria. In many cases it is not clear why schools included those additional children. They did not all have parental records of difficulties experienced at school, nor of difficulties in learning and/or behaviour. It appears that schools used their own knowledge to enter these pupils. One explanation is that schools included children who were already on their own register, for example because they had asthma or another medical condition irrespective of whether the parents reported an impact.

Of the 36 schools who entered these data, 16 had reported differences to the research team, but in the majority of cases these were limited to four children or less. Closer scrutiny revealed that five schools (three primary and two secondary) accounted for 84 (81 per cent) of the additional children.

'Allen' secondary school entered data from 24 of the 110 returned questionnaires in the school census. Three of these pupils met the criteria for inclusion. There were an additional 21 children entered, none of whom was reported to experience a substantial impact. Eleven parents had indicated their child had a physical or mental health condition, impairment or difficulty, and that this had gone on for a long time. A further parent was unsure if their child had a condition. Two further children had experienced an accident or trauma, one of which was too recent to have led to a long-standing impact. None of these additional children experienced an impact.

On the one hand the degree of difference between schools' entries on the census and that of the research team is surprising especially given that schools reported the sifting to be an easy and straightforward process. However four of the five schools with the greatest disparity were not able to attend briefing meetings and may therefore have been unclear about the rationale for entering data *only* from children that met the criteria or, perhaps more likely, that despite the guidance, they were unclear about the pivotal role of impact. In the busy life of the school guidance may not be on hand at the point at which the data are entered.

> 'Morris' primary school had returns from 123 children, they entered 24 children in the online census of which 23 did not match the guidance for inclusion. None of these additional children was reported by their parents to experience an impact although seven parents reported 'occasionally it interferes with everyday activities, but only in a minor way'. Sixteen answered yes their child had a mental or physical health condition but did not fulfil any of the additional criteria. There appeared to be no consistent pattern to explain why these children were viewed as meeting the criteria.

Schools therefore were inclined to over-identify disabled pupils – a criticism that has also been made in relation to special educational needs (DfE 2011a; Lamb 2009; Ofsted 2010). The argument in relation to special educational needs is that in part it reflects the definition – that children require provision that is additional to and different from that which is currently available and consequently reflects the quality of the general offer. However it is likely that there are more complex issues at work here and, as Lamb (2011) points out, these include the perverse incentives of 'the contextual value-added scores, mislabelling children who have simply fallen behind, lagging performance of summer-born children ... the level of SEN support in a school, differing definitions of what constitutes inadequate progress, catchment area and local policies adopted'. One of the fundamental concerns that is particularly relevant here is that over-identification can reduce the expectations of those children.

Conclusion

Schools' responses suggested that the data collected provided a more detailed and fuller picture of the experiences of the child. In providing a more holistic picture schools became aware of some children whose needs had previously been invisible to them. This was particularly true where children managed their health condition through staying at home when the symptoms were particularly acute. Despite the presence of children who were not on the school's radar, in general there was a tendency to over-identify disabled children. While on the one hand this reveals a willingness to be alert to the difficulties experienced by children. On the other hand, at least for some schools, it suggests that they don't understand the fundamental role of impact and in consequence what disability really means. Without taking on board the contextual nature of disability, these schools run the risk of assigning the child's difficulties to their impairment or health condition, failing to recognize the ways in which the school contributed to their experience of participation. We would hope that schools would look particularly at whether these children are achieving in line with their expectations and to their overall wellbeing.

The return rates of some schools are a matter of concern. Taking the schools with the lowest rates, these were more likely to be in areas of deprivation with higher proportions of children eligible for free school meals. This is a particular issue given the two-way relationship between poverty and disability in children 'with a close geographical dimension' (IPPR 2007) so that children who are particularly disadvantaged may be under-represented in both school and local authority statistics through low return rates. It should however be recognized that eligibility for free school meals has been critiqued as a measure of disadvantage (Gorard 2012; Kounali et al. (submitted for publication); Lauder et al. 2010) but this does not undermine the link between return rates, disability and this group of children.

Elsewhere we have also raised some concern that the returns under-represented children with mental health conditions (Porter et al. 2011) The Mental Health Survey suggests one in ten children aged 5–16 have a clinically diagnosed mental disorder (Green et al. 2005). This figure exceeds that quoted for *all* children with a disability of around 7 per cent (DfES and DRC 2006). Notably Grant and Hamlyn (2008/9), in the returns for their study of services for disabled children, found 15 per cent of 16–19 year olds suffer from depression. In the light of this under-reporting this survey tool made explicit reference to mental health needs in the opening phrasing of all relevant questions. Over one in five children who met the disability criteria were described by their parents as having anxiety or depression. Notably almost a third of children identified as disabled in secondary schools had a mental health need. Few however were recorded as having mental health needs only, with the vast majority having those needs in combination with others. These are difficult data to evaluate. Green et al. (2005) report an overall incidence of clinical mental health difficulties in children 5–16 to be 9.6 per cent but this includes children with conduct disorders who would be represented elsewhere in our survey. Looking just at emotional disorders the national prevalence is 3.7 per cent, with a slightly higher incidence in girls. This group is under-represented in this survey as it formed just over 2 per cent of our sample. Disclosure by children that they are struggling with aspects of school life have a higher reported incidence than those reported by their parents (Porter *et al.* 2008) and it is probable that children provide a more transparent account of their emotional difficulties than parents, reinforcing the importance of schools collecting data directly from children as well as parents.

Chapter 7

From understanding to responding

Introduction

This final chapter draws together the findings of our research to consider the implications both in relation to school policy and practices and in the wider context of collecting disability data. It revisits the place of a rights-based approach and argues that, despite the challenges, schools are better placed to engage with the meaning of disability through meeting their disability equality duties. In consequence the data support a better understanding of the nature of disabling experiences and are enabled to respond proactively to offset these. These understandings are set within the overwhelming view of children of schools as social institutions. What defines participation is the presence of others. What both supports and hinders participation are the relationships formed with others – peers and staff. What makes participation good is the sense of belonging. Conversely, the experience of being disconnected denies children opportunities for learning and for being part of the community. The collection of disability data enables schools to monitor their effectiveness in achieving this – to go beyond the rhetoric laid down in plans and schemes and provide evidence that they are meeting the needs of all children. This extends the customary narrow definition of achievement to reflect Terzi's (2007) stance on the importance of developing capabilities: people's freedom to achieve their own wellbeing, opportunities to choose what they can do or become – the 'pre-requisites for an equal participation in society' (p. 758).

There are also wider implications of our research for the way that data are collected. Our approach to the collection revealed important gaps in current practice – not least the disconnect in mainstream schools between disability and special educational needs, and the limitations of using the latter as a single proxy measure. The data have revealed the pivotal role of impact in understanding disability and contribute further evidence for understanding that disability is contextually and culturally situated, and can only be understood and responded to in that light. Schools therefore play a vital role in enabling young people to have the freedom to choose to live the life that they value. There are however a number of challenges to achieving this. Equity, like inclusion, are not end states: 'they are things to be struggled towards and struggled over' (Ball 2013, p. 40). What will be outlined here are some of the many steps along the way.

Disability is a global concern, and while some have asked about the extent to which a social model is applicable outside developed countries (Shakespeare 2012), there has been a worldwide recognition of the rights of disabled people and of their inequitable access to resources and opportunities (World Health Organization and World Bank 2011). This book has its origins in research funded to enable schools to meet their duties under the Equality Act 2010 and its predecessors. Its premise was one of ensuring equity in provision for disabled children, enabling schools to make the first steps in collecting their own data that would enable them to make informed decisions about the adjustments that would enhance participation – in all aspects of schooling. Its central premise was closing the gap between pupils' rights 'on paper' and how they are experienced on the ground. Disability however appears to be disappearing from the UK government agenda. There was little mention of the Disability Discrimination Acts in the Green Paper, and the Equality Act revealed a reduction in the Public Sector Equality Duties. This comes at a time where disabled children are at an increased risk. The impact of the recession and cuts are experienced disproportionately on disabled children and their family (Larkins *et al.* 2013). As the Children's Commissioner for England states: 'One of the most significant barriers to the inclusion of disabled children in society is poverty' (OCC 2012, p. 21). She makes two recommendations which are particularly pertinent to the work here:

> R54 Data should be gathered on the number of children affected by disability and the nature of this disability. This will enable the UK Government and devolved administrations, local authorities and health boards to plan services for disabled children and their families more effectively.
>
> (OCC 2011, p. 23)

This recommendation is followed by one that address concerns about 'the major gaps in service provision and outcomes for disabled children' and includes:

> R61 The UK Government and devolved administrations should measure attainment levels of disabled children, not just in terms of grades achieved but whether they are making progress towards reaching their potential.
>
> (OCC 2011, p. 24)

Although the statutory requirements on schools have lessened, legislation still provides an important safeguard for parents and children and it is this we can utilize to promote an understanding of the meaning of disability and provide the catalyst for change.

While there can be many criticisms that a rights-based approach perpetuates the notion of an individual problem and fails to change society (Finkelstein 2007) it still provides fertile ground for developing a framework for action. It legitimates demands for a fairer system, one that does not necessarily mean treating everyone the same but instead concerns the pursuit of equity. Moreover it is important that this major achievement is not abandoned simply because it's seen to be too 'burdensome' to implement. Rather than arguing that the process of data collection, and publishing disability schemes, are unnecessarily bureaucratic, engagement with these processes provides a better understanding of disability and a consideration of how schools should respond. This reflects the comments made during the course of our studies. This was not simply collecting data for data sake. As one local authority adviser in our study said: 'schools' thinking changed as a result of the questionnaire'. A number of staff commented on how it provides 'more detailed knowledge'. It gets people 'to think more deeply about the ... definition of disability'. It challenged schools' assumptions that disability equates to special educational needs – that all disabled children experienced difficulties in learning.

The use of a survey tool such as the parent questionnaire surfaces a number of tensions. One of the uncertainties that schools voice is the risk of making disabled pupils feel different to others through the process of identification. It can be argued that if we don't run that risk then we cannot be sure that we are acting proactively, ensuring equity in access to the full range of opportunities in our provision. As Norwich (2008) states: 'the problem of inequality can be aggravated either by treating members of a minority as the same as the majority or by treating them as different' (p. 8). Treating people differently can serve to emphasize differences and treating them the same can prove equally insensitive. The allocation of equal resources serves to maintain disadvantage yet is also argued to be a fair system. Of course Norwich (2008) was writing in the context of special educational needs when he discussed the dilemmas that are faced. One vital difference with respect to disability is that the latter is based on self-disclosure. While professionals may diagnose the presence of a mental or physical health condition, the extent to which the experience is disabling is determined by the person themselves. They therefore have an important choice of whether identification has benefits or not. It is the professionals' role to provide them with this opportunity to decide and an environment that empowers them to do so.

Alongside the issue of identification is one of thresholds, and a reluctance to base these around subjective experience. Notably the World Health Organization, in producing its detailed international framework, refrained from suggesting cut-off points. This was viewed as a government issue tied to the allocation of resources. In taking this stance, the organization avoided the political issue of who is worthy of special resources and who is not. Some schools voiced a dilemma to us about the resource implications of identifying 'more' children who may have unmet needs. This presumes that there is a cost implication of the adjustments that might be necessary – one that is over and above that of changing attitudes and appreciating the implications of equity by allowing some flexibility in the enforcement of rules and procedures. There is also a further element in recognizing the centrality of impact – as a subjective experience. Commonly used objective disability measures such as 'ability to walk 100 metres' fail to capture differences between individuals in the pain, time and effort to undertake that activity, or the risks that it involves or whether this ability is integral to valued activities and participation. It also fails to take into account the availability of supports and the presence of barriers to achievement. Experiential data are likely to provide schools with some surprises and the need to reassess their knowledge base. It can engender recognition of the need for different modes of communication with parents and children.

The implications of adopting an interactive stance

The field of disability has been dominated by passionate arguments and oppositional standpoints. Not surprisingly, given the importance of the topic, writers express strong and sometimes vitriolic views, and there is little middle ground in education that combines medical and social standpoints (Norwich 2012). This research took an interactive position, adopting the definition by Shakespeare (2006), but mindful of the criticisms that have been directed at it. These criticisms largely concern the couching of the model within a critique of the social model (as evidenced in the reviews of Sheldon *et al.* 2007). This is not the context in which the approach was adopted here. Rather the strengths of the social model were recognized, raising awareness of the discriminatory practices that are at work and the need for responses to be empowering, supporting children to be active agents in the process of change. These tenets were built on using a relational social model to understand the dual way in which oppression occurs, both externally through the structures and systems of organizations and individuals and through the internalization of these values and practices.

In order to navigate a path through this terrain we adopted a two-pronged approach to the process of data collection – with both elements making a necessary contribution to enabling schools to respond both proactively, in anticipation, by removing barriers for disabled children, and reactively to support their participation. We developed two types of tool, one that collected data from parents in a structured and prescribed way and the other that collected the views of children in a flexible manner, adaptable to the local context. In this way schools could collect data from parents that could be aggregated and shared with local authorities and government, enabling them also to monitor the impact of their policies and procedures. We shunned the approach that had been typically developed for adult populations of a two-stage question for one that invited parents to respond more thoughtfully about their child's experiences of participation using multiple indicators of disability, ones that hinged around a pivotal question of the degree of impact. Our second approach, the flexible tools, were embedded within guidance to schools on providing an ethos in which it's OK to be different, to find some elements of participation tricky. The tools were designed to be used flexibly and the findings to be understood in the context of the way the views were collected and used to inform policy and practice at the local level. There was a universaility to the approach that embraced *all* children rather than targeting a few. Our concern was to enable schools to be aware that some children's conditions are rendered invisible through absences and the development of coping mechanisms that may limit the opportunity to fully participate in all school activities.

Through using the parent questionnaire schools were able to understand what the definition provided by the Equality Act meant in practice. Schools were given guidance on analyzing responses to the questionnaire to identify children who met the legal criteria and the application of this to their own data enabled them to recognize that impairment did not inevitably lead to disability. For some this will have been a steep learning curve from a prior position of equating disability to children in wheelchairs. Many schools learned of children whose disability had previously been invisible to them. Often this was because they were unaware of a health condition or did not understand its impact. They were not aware of the strategies children used to manage their condition. It was in many instances the start of what parents have said they find so useful – a 'listening conversation' (Stobbs 2012).

It was the open question where parents were asked about what their child found particularly supportive that provided schools with the greatest insights. In responding to this question parents took the opportunity to explain aspects of their child's experiences. Schools gained important information that enabled them to understand the child's participation in school better: the child not sleeping and the impact on behaviour, the effect of absences on the child's confidence, the stressful effect of something new or different. In this way schools were also supported in understanding why particular actions on their behalf were helpful (or not). Many parents also responded by writing about the way that learning was organized and in particular how important one-to-one support or the presence of a teaching assistant was for their child. One analysis of this, consistent with parent comments, is that these members of staff were seen to provide the 'soft skills – confidence and motivation, dispositions towards learning' (Webster *et al.* 2010, p. 331). This was especially true for parents of mainstream primary children where having someone 'dedicated' to looking out for their child was valued. We should not however assume that this leads to better individualized learning as this runs contrary to other evidence, nor that it presumes that children are enabled to participate in activities (Blatchford *et al.* 2009; Symes and Humphrey 2012; Webster and Blatchford 2013), rather it ensures attention to their child. This resonates well with the overriding concerns of parents for someone who understands their child's needs that was so apparent in the evidence to the Lamb Inquiry (2009).

In secondary schools the descriptions of support from parents shifted from someone being there to the nature of the relationship with adults – the importance of being understood, especially for children with mental health needs. Strategies by which schools were able to be flexible in their responses, waiving rules and regulations when necessary, were particularly welcomed. Notably parents were much less likely to write about aspects of the curriculum or about particular teaching approaches – reinforcing the importance of seeing schools as social institutions.

This element was reinforced in the views of children. The data reveal that it is the social aspects of schooling that impinge on children. Consistent with parents' responses, younger children valued contact with adults, and for older children it was the quality of the contact that was important. However it was often the informal aspects of school life that pupils referred to. In primary schools this included the times and places that called most on children's social skills and where they looked to both peers and adults for support. In secondary schools the overriding message is of the importance of relationships, both as a barrier and as a source of immense support. Friends featured in the comments of children in a way that was largely absent in the responses from parents. Friends form a buffer in the face of difficulties. Having someone to look out for you and support you enables you to deal with the negative behaviour of others. The transition from adult support to peer support rests on the development of friendships and the responses of primary aged children revealed how many children find it difficult to make friends.

When children were given the equivalent of a magic wand those in secondary schools were most likely to change some element of their social relationships, either the behaviour of other children or that of staff. In primary school disabled children were more likely to write about lessons and activities – things they found too hard. Disabled children were more than twice as likely to use their wand to change the behaviour of bullies than their non-disabled peers. This is consistent with research elsewhere that suggests that bullying is a particular problem experienced by this group (Blake *et al.* 2012; Connors and Stalker 2002; Naylor *et al.* 2012; Pellegrini 2002).

It was notable that when children were asked if they had a difficulty or disability around one in five indicated that they thought they did. There were marked differences between schools in these rates. This further reinforces the importance of listening to children, to providing them with a space in which to express their concerns and challenges.

Making data collection manageable for schools

During the two phases of this project it became evident which of the many practices supported schools in the process of data collection. The purpose had been to devise user-friendly tools and to help schools in meeting clear deadlines in a timely manner. In the second phase in particular our aim had been to mimic the stages that would be required by a national annual school census. To this end we briefed schools on how to maximize return rates and provided them with the materials and exemplars to do so. We concluded that there were clear advantages to using an online rather than a paper-based method, one that is shared where data are entered and where there is a system in place for the analysis of which children meet the Equality Act criteria. This reduces the demands on schools while ensuring that all schools are producing comparative data. However as we learned only a small percentage of parents, when given the choice, complete a questionnaire online. A further concern was that schools had a variable response rate to the questionnaires, and in general terms those in areas of deprivation, where there are likely to be more disabled children, had the lowest return rates (although there were schools who defied this generality by achieving a higher than average return rate). It would therefore seem logical to link the process of data collection to a time when schools already collect data from all parents – admissions. In this way response rates are more likely to be uniformly high, and those parents who require help to complete the questionnaire can be supported. However it should be recognized that parents may feel less confident in talking about their child's difficulties before they have built a relationship with the school. They may in particular not wish to create a self-fulfilling prophecy nor put their child's place in jeopardy. This issue therefore needs to be handled with sensitivity and be embodied in a wider agenda of the school's response to diversity and difference. The school response to diversity will also impact later when the data will need to be 'refreshed' during the course of attendance at school. Schools routinely ask parents to let them know about changes in address, contact details and medication but asking about disability requires more precision. We would anticipate that this would involve using the full questionnaire to ensure a proper opportunity for a 'listening conversation'. Where schools are relying on data managers they need to ensure that they have appropriate briefing and are aware of the confidential nature of the information.

The spirit of the Act however will be denied if schools are not also supported to collect the views of children. Here of course the timing of admissions is probably inappropriate. If asked teachers would likely say they routinely collect the views of children, that it is integral to their practice within classrooms. However talking with children about the challenges to participation is rather different to discussion that focuses on the curriculum. Discussion in class usually takes place within the context of teachers having expert knowledge, where the direction of conversations are familiar, where the objective has already been formulated and the agenda set. In contrast teachers may feel much less prepared for open discussions that involve sensitive issues and emotional challenges. It is perhaps unsurprising that teachers chose structured methods from the tool kit, ones where the content was predetermined and could be 'administered' to large groups of pupils. This may reflect the constraints of time, and the efficiency of finding out from many children. It also often involved anonymous methods.

On the one hand this enabled children to respond without needing to anticipate how the information would be received. On the other hand it also provided teachers with the space to reflect on how to respond. The guidance we provided to schools suggested that it was not necessarily teachers who were best placed to collect this information, however this is not to deny their responsibility for responding and suggestions for developing school practices need to be framed in a way that promotes ownership.

Implications for school practice and policy

The parameters of the project precluded a more detailed examination of the ways in which schools changed as a result of new knowledge and understanding and how this was received. Instead I explore the implications of the way forward, reflecting on the overwhelming evidence of the importance of the relational nature of disability and the social elements of schooling. Increasingly during the school years interactions with peers are the bedrock of what it means to participate in school, reinforcing the interdependence of learning, relating and belonging. Relationships both with peers as well as teachers affect young people's feelings of connectedness to the school, and the converse, that is poor relationships and connectedness put young people at risk. Friendships in particular have, as MacArthur (2013) states, been an under-recognized dimension of schooling and one largely ignored by policy-makers. She quotes Morris (2002): 'from children's point of view, friendship is the main motivation for going to school and that difficulties with making and maintaining friendships are a key barrier to getting the most out of education.' This resonates well with our findings. Children who do not find it easy to form friendships do not have a source of comfort to help them cope with crises. Addressing aspects of interaction, peer–peer, staff–pupil and parent–staff, are central to schools' responses to disability.

It was notable that many of the barriers were shared by a number of children – children who are struggling and experiencing difficulty will not necessarily meet the legislative definition of disability. Some of these barriers are amenable to quick and easy adjustments. Proximity to the teacher offsets some of the difficulties caused by poor acoustics making it easier to attend and contribute. Forewarning of changes in routine removes some of the stresses of unanticipated events. Management of passage in crowded spaces reduces the likelihood of poor interactions, pushing, teasing and name-calling. Sitting close enough to friends to support a sense of belonging or, as one pupil wrote, '*If people could sit near enough to friends to be comfortable but not so close that they would be distracted*'.

These are really the starting points for considering change. They largely concern managing the situation better, rather than being enabling or empowering. Moreover we can make an important distinction between being responsive and being proactive. The former relates to responding to a particular individual's needs, developing the systems and structures that support this process. The other concerns developing the culture in which these changes take place. Arguably, given the diversity of experiences, neither can exist in isolation.

Communication lies at the heart of the changes. The recent evaluation of a national pilot of the Achievement for All programme (Humphrey and Squires 2011) has highlighted the importance of schools having regular structured conversations with parents and that these together with more effective use of data on assessment, tracking and intervention and provision for wider outcomes has led to a greater emphasis on understanding pupils' needs and a significant improvement in relationships including reductions in bullying. Structured conversations enabled teachers to 'change their expectations of pupils and recognize the full potential of pupils' (Humphrey and Squires 2011, p. 14). The evaluators also suggest that the attitudes of teachers changed so that they saw greater teacher responsibility for children with SEND rather than leaving them to the teaching assistant. They conclude that schools should be aiming to have at least two structured conversations with parents in a year. The evaluation provides optimism about the potential for a real culture change within schools.

However the success of interventions can have a differential impact. Another high-profile intervention project concerning the development of social skills and relationships – an area pertinent to our findings – has been withdrawn. The Social and Emotional Learning project (Humphrey et al. 2010) uses a 'loose framework' for supporting schools in enabling pupils to develop self-awareness, self-regulation (managing feelings), motivation, empathy, social skills. The evaluation reveals the challenge of bringing about widespread improvements in this area of development, with schools implementing the programme to differing degrees with a mixed result (Humphrey et al. 2010). Schools take-up and interpretation of the programme is an important factor in contributing to its impact. In consequence it was successful in individual schools with a differential impact on different groups of children. Notably one evaluation (Hallam 2009) argues for the importance of involving parents. In contrast a programme with a tighter framework designed to manage anxiety suggests that there are other factors at work in the success of widespread interventions. Stallard and colleagues (submitted for publication) have recently carried out randomized control trials of a programme entitled FRIENDS designed to help pupils develop strategies for reducing anxiety. The programme has been trialled in primary schools to help pupils develop the skills 'to confront and cope with anxiety provoking events' with promising results. Of significance here are the early day findings of the effect of the school culture on the success of the programme (Skryabina 2014). Typically researchers look for school effects using secondary data with measures such as size, numbers of pupils on free school meals, and percentage of pupils with SEN. Unusually this study has developed measures based on the school pedagogic practices including the emphasis placed on academic versus social attainment, who selects, sequences and paces the work. Such approaches may go some way to explain why programmes typically have a differential impact with more subtle and complex influences at work. In the FRIENDS study the intervention was least effective in academic schools, and most effective for boys where schools placed equal emphasis on academic and social and emotional development (Skyrabina 2014). We cannot consider interventions without therefore thinking about the school community.

Shaping the community

Schools have an important and proactive role in shaping the community both inside and outside the school gates – it's not simply about meeting the needs of the individual child. Beckett and Buckner (2012) argue that the role of staff goes beyond ensuring equal access to opportunities and experiences for disabled children. They need to support all children to recognize and think critically about disempowering discourses as they relate to all protected characteristics – bringing to the fore that disability is a public rather than an individual issue. However schools in turn need supporting to achieve this. Beckett and Buckner's data suggest that some three in ten schools have a plan to promote positive attitudes, with just over half recognizing that they could do more. In fact they suggest that it is the 'poor relation' compared with race and gender. Staff when interviewed replied that there just wasn't time. They felt they had few resources to draw on other than the children themselves. Notably those schools with high levels of children with SEN were less likely to have resources including books with disabled characters. They raise the challenge of inspiring teachers to be creative in their teaching when there has been a narrowing of the curriculum and a pressure to constantly raise achievement against a narrow set of indicators.

Beckett (2013), in a study of non-disabled primary school children's view of disability, provides compelling further evidence of the need for schools to do more. Children revealed an individual model in their responses to being asked about disability, an issue that was a problem for the person as their bodies did not work properly rather than a public issue. More encouragingly the older children did argue for the importance of being treated fairly. Staff discourse is a powerful mediator not just in directly impacting on children's own sense of identity but also in providing a model of how others should interact. This is not to infer intentionality on their behalf. In some instances it may reflect the overriding concerns to cover the curriculum in a limited time frame. Staff may also lack skills in communicating with disabled children. The Children's Commissioner (OCC 2011) has recently raised concerns about the variable extent to which staff are prepared and able to communicate with disabled pupils. Naraian (2011) illustrates the importance of teacher talk in developing the identity of a child with significant impairments, Harry, as the teacher mediates between him and his peers. It illustrates how on the one hand the teacher can be vigilant in promoting acceptance and encouraging interaction and respect, but on the other fail to promote understanding or a meaningful relationship.

In many ways the case study teacher was observed using a number of com-mendable practices: drawing the child into activities, structuring opportunities for him to work with different partners, enabling him to take part in activities. There was however no sense in which the children were encouraged to explore their experiences with disabled children to make sense or understand Harry's responses. They remained uncertain about speaking on behalf of, or making inferences about his wishes. By avoiding tricky conversations, the teacher limited the relationships they could have with him as well as constraining the development of his own sense of agency.

What is required goes beyond the acquisition of skills, or the delivery of content. It requires much more than schools 'ticking the boxes' that are necessary to meet the standards of inspection. A technical approach which is so characteristic of policy and practice may fail to tackle institutions as social organizations. It may in particular overlook the issue of pupil–teacher relationships which appear to be as central in the everyday experience of young people in contributing to emotional wellbeing. On the other hand, as others have indicated, the imperative to consider and respond to these challenging issues can easily be lost as the spotlight falls on other more measureable aspects of school performance. Robinson (2009) has drawn attention to the mismatch that can exist between policy-makers and implementors in their understanding of the theories or explanations that underpin the policy. Here it is a fundamental requirement that schools engage with the philosophy to bring about a culture change. It was evident in some schools in our project that they had a narrowly conceived view of disability, and a low expectation of communicating with parents. Robinson (2009) suggests that open-ended policy innovations, while giving good space for teacher creativity, can result in no actual change in behaviour and consequently no impact. Surprisingly more structured and prescriptive interventions had the greatest impact. It is therefore regretful that the obligations on schools have been reduced, that the necessity for collecting disability data has moved from being a voluntary aspect of the school census to not featuring at all. SEN data however continue to be collected. Rather than removing the obligation and leaving the means and the methods open to schools it is clear that there are many virtues to a more prescriptive approach – providing it is manageable for schools.

A prescriptive approach however does not sit easily with government policy of devolvement of responsibilities to schools with growing numbers freed from local authority control. Rather it is left to schools to decide whether or not they collect these data. The values that underpin this work are at odds with the current marketization and commodification of education, where some pupils may be seen as resource intensive. Parents and children are differentially placed when it comes to exercising their right to choice of schools. Against this tide however there are voices of dissent.

In a recent policy paper for the Centre for Labour and Social Studies, Ball (2013), with a rather broader focus of disadvantage, has argued for the need to consider more radical reforms to address the increasing inequalities, developing new cultures for recognizing diversity.

> Essentially, tackling the relationship between education, inequality and poverty differently would involve re-connecting education with the lives, hopes and aspirations of children and parents, not through choice and competition but through participation, debate and educative engagement of schools with their communities.
>
> (Ball 2013, p. 35)

He argues for the development of new forums for communication so that parents and children, as well as wider community stakeholders, contribute to social change. This echoes the work of Fielding and others in calls for a more radical and transformatory education where democratic processes lie at the core (Fielding and Moss 2011). It is a timely reminder that as we take steps along the path to a more equitable society there are bigger visions of what this would look like. Arguably disability data collection is an early step along that path.

Implications for disability data collection

The data from the study have wider implications for disability data collection. The development of the tools revealed the necessity of developing appropriate instruments for collecting information about children rather than starting with adult versions and making adjustments. By doing this we were able to devise questions that prompted engagement with participation as a starting point from which to later reflect on impact. We were able to draw on studies that demonstrate the power of language in enabling parents to understand the relevance of the questions. In particular, providing a clear context for the collection of the data enabled parents to understand the purpose and utility of responding. 'Making schools better places for learning' was an appropriate caption for this work.

The data from the parent questionnaire revealed the dramatic fall in numbers of children with the application in turn of each of the criteria of the Equality Act. The presence of a health condition or impairment, that has gone on for a year or more (or is expected to), that has a substantial impact on daily life each reduced the number of children identified. In doing so it revealed the limitations of measures that fail to make these distinctions, and further exemplified the disparity in rates that result from different survey devices. Moreover the survey explicitly included those children who are easily overlooked; those who have suffered a physical or mental trauma that has an enduring impact. Although our survey suggests the numbers of children are small, their inclusion is important if we are to take the definition of disability seriously.

During the piloting of our questionnaire it became apparent that measures of impact needed to be meaningful and invite consideration. They needed to reflect the fluidity and contextual nature of disability. This can be contrasted to the rather generic approach used in recent Office of National Statistic surveys of 'no impact, a little or a lot'. In order to help parents consider their response to impact questions, they were asked about the child's participation in school, home and community settings, thereby supporting a holistic appraisal of impact. For the purposes of clarification with other government measures we also included questions relating to the child's needs and functioning but voiced concerns at the time that such questions provided a catalogue from which to describe deficits, unbalanced by any acknowledgement of strengths (Porter *et al.* 2008). Again the data revealed the importance of not inferring that these measures always equate to impact. Like others have found, severity of a condition does not predict the effect (Dickinson *et al.* 2007; White-Koning *et al.* 2005), although there is also some evidence from international studies to suggest that support systems and schools influence participation patterns (Ullenhag *et al.* 2012). In particular this points to the importance of further understanding the ways in which culture and context impact on the experience of disability.

Finally we turn to the disconnect in the data between disability and special educational needs. Across the board SEN has been used as a proxy measure, in large part probably because they are data that schools have and report to LAs and government. While having the advantage of convenience it fails to recognize or safeguard some 50 per cent of disabled children in mainstream schools who don't have SEN. It demonstrates the importance of freeing identification of disability from (specialist) service provision and focusing instead on making universal systems fit for purpose. Simply equating disability with special educational needs leaves a large number of children to 'fall through the gap'. It perpetuates a belief that the only concern that schools should have is achievement, that wellbeing and participation should not form part of their agenda. It denies the strong message evident in our data of the connection between learning, relationships and belonging.

Conclusion

The data have illustrated the ways in which disability can be seen as a culturally situated construct where the effect of the impairment is mediated by the adjustments and supports available in both the home and school settings. Two levels of responsiveness can be identified: the first being one which operates in the interface between a particular child and the school and/or particular teachers, and the second that exists between the school and the national culture which results in a local situated understanding of the nature, extent and implications of impairment and disability; this conditions the way in which the school and/or the teachers' attention is directed towards or deflected away from the nature, extent and implications of the barriers to progress that may be experienced by the child; the availability of supports impact on whether a child is disabled or not. The culture of the school shapes the nature of that support and the way it is experienced. A child with a number of different areas of need may only occasionally experience an impairment as a disability, another with a single area of need may experience the impact daily. This creates an unusual and fluid context in which to collect and report data. As schools learn from children and their parents about the ways in which they can best be supported fewer children will be reported as disabled. Moreover schools will become more sensitive to the needs of children whose coping strategies have enabled them to remain invisible to schools. They are therefore important data to collect and not just for schools but also local authorities and government whose policies and procedures can have an adverse effect on the daily lives of children.

The challenge of uncertainty, fluidity and contextuality in conceptualizing disability creates a complex dynamic that could also easily, and worryingly, result in the homogenization of the experience of disability (Davis and Watson 2002), where children are slotted into categories based on the degree or type of 'reasonable adjustments' that are required. The effectiveness of the legislation depends in part on schools understanding the pivotal role of impact and being informed about this in the analysis and reporting of data. In particular schools need to understand the ways in which children deal with different health conditions in school as this is central to ensuring that schools are well placed to make reasonable adjustments and ensure equality of opportunity. The sensitivity of these data highlights the need for schools to be proactive in assuring parents and children of the ways in which these data will be used and the steps that will be taken to respect confidentiality. Developing a culture that promotes participation, values diversity and does not use single measures of achievement as markers of its success are important steps towards achieving social justice for disabled children.

Appendix

Making schools better places for learning

Please help us find out about any physical or mental health condition, disability or difficulty that may affect your child's learning. We have a legal duty to take steps to improve outcomes for disabled people. The information will be used by us to promote the wellbeing of disabled children and address any difficulties they face in all aspects of school life.

Please take the time to answer all questions and return the form <u>whether or not your child has any difficulties</u>. Please complete one form for each of your children at this school.

We will treat what you have told us here sensitively. None of the information will be shared with other parents or pupils. The back page of this questionnaire provides more information about who this information will be shared with. If you need help to fill in this questionnaire please let us know.

Child's first name	Child's surname / family name
....	....
Child's other names	Date of birth (dd/mm/yy) ../ .. / ..
....	
Gender (please circle): Boy	Girl

1. **Does your child have any difficulty that affects his or her:**

	Yes	Sometimes	No	Don't know
a) Classroom learning?				
b) Interaction with his or her classmates / peers?				
c) Joining in other school activities e.g. lunchtimes, breaks, social and leisure activities in school?				

2. **Does your child have any difficulty that affects his or her:**

	Yes	Sometimes	No
a) Daily activities such as eating, dressing, communicating, moving around, going to the toilet?			
b) Taking a full part in activities at home?			
c) Taking part in activities outside the home?			

3. **Does your child have a difficulty which means that they are sometimes absent from school?**

☐ Yes   ☐ No

4.   **Has your child had an accident or psychological trauma (e.g. loss of someone close) in the last 5 years that has seriously limited their activities either at home or school?**

☐ Yes   ☐ No

If yes please describe:	If more than one incident please describe:
Month/year it happened:	Month/year it happened:
............../...........	............../.................

5.i) **Does your child have a physical or mental health condition, impairment or difficulty such as: anxiety or depression, arthritis, asthma, autism, cancer, diabetes, epilepsy, hearing or visual impairment, HIV, Chronic Fatigue Syndrome (ME), mental health difficulty, mobility problems, learning difficulty, physical difficulties or a severe disfigurement?**

☐ Yes   ☐ No   ☐ Unsure

If you answered yes:

5.ii) **Has the physical or mental health condition, impairment or difficulty gone on for a year or more (or is it likely to)?**

☐ Yes   ☐ No   ☐ Unsure

If you answered Yes to any of the questions 1 to 5 please go to question 6 overleaf.

If not please go to question 11 on the last page.

---

6. **Has your child seen a professional (e.g. paediatrician, psychologist) because of the physical or mental health condition, impairment or difficulty?**

☐ Yes   ☐ No

> If yes **please circle** who you have seen:
> educational psychologist / doctor / counsellor / paediatrician / therapist
>
> Other (please specify):
>
> What was the condition identified / diagnosed?

7. **Overall, how does the physical or mental health condition, impairment or difficulty (when taken together) affect your child in their daily life? (Please tick one only)**

a) No difficulty. My child can take a full part in home, community and school activities	
b) Occasionally it interferes with everyday activities but only in a *minor* way – there is an impact but it is trivial or small	
c) There are particular times and situations when activities are regularly stopped or limited because of the difficulty	
d) It frequently affects a number of daily activities	
e) The impact is felt on almost all activities every day	

8. **How is your child affected as a result of their physical or mental health condition, impairment or difficulty? Please tick any that apply to your child.**

a) Mobility: getting around in or outside the home	
b) Hand function: holding and touching	
c) Personal care: has difficulty washing, going to the toilet, dressing	
d) Eating and drinking: has difficulty eating or drinking by themselves or sickness or lack of appetite	
e) Incontinence: has difficulty controlling the passage of urine and/or faeces	
f) Communication: speaking and /or understanding others	
g) Learning: has special educational needs	
h) Hearing	
i) Vision	
j) Behaviour: has a condition that leads to the child being hyperactive or having a short attention span or getting frustrated or behaving in a socially unacceptable manner	
k) Consciousness: has fits or seizures	
l) Diagnosed with Autism, Asperger Syndrome or Autistic Spectrum Disorder (ASD)	
m) Palliative care needs	
n) Mental health needs e.g. depression, anxiety, eating disorder, OCD	
o) Recognising when they are in physical danger, e.g. crossing the road, jumping from heights	
p) Other (please write in any other area(s) that your child is affected)	

9.i) **Does your child take any medication, use any physical aids or require any special diet or supplements for any physical or mental health condition, impairment or difficulty? Please tick any that apply to your child.**

a) No medication, physical aids or diets	
b) Yes – Medication (including inhaler)	
c) Yes – Physical aids (including hearing and walking aids but NOT glasses)	
d) Yes - Special diet or supplement	

If you answered yes:

9.ii) **Without these would your child's health problem(s) (when taken together) substantially affect their life?**

☐   Yes   ☐   No

10. **Please describe the support that your child finds particularly helpful to enable them to take part in daily activities in school, at home or in the community e.g. access to therapy, computers, respite care, support from friends, skills training.**

11. If you have not already had an opportunity would you like to talk about any of these issues with a member of school staff?

☐ Yes   ☐ No

What happens to the information you give us?

We really appreciate your help with this questionnaire. The information will be used by the school to improve the way that information on disability is collected and used in schools to promote the wellbeing of children. No information will be published that would identify your child. By returning this form you are agreeing that information can be used in this way. The covering letter shows the person in the school who will open the envelope and see this information. Information will be shared with those staff in the school who support your child unless you ask us not to below

Is there any person in the school who you <u>would not</u> like to share this information with?
Please name them : ....

Please return the form to your school in the envelope provided by XXXX

Many thanks for taking the time to fill in this form.

Bibliography

Abberley, P. (1987) The concept of oppression and the development of a social theory of disability. *Disability, Handicap and Society*, 2(1), 5–19.

——(1992) Counting us out: a discussion of the OPCS disability surveys. *Disability, Handicap and Society*, 7(2), 139–155.

Advisory Committee on Australian and International Disability Data (2005) *Collecting Disability Data: A Guide for Service Providers*. Data Starter 2 Australian Institute of Health and Welfare.

Ainscow, M. (2007) From special education to effective schools for all: a review of progress so far, in L. Florian (ed.) *The Sage Handbook of Special Education*. London: Sage, pp. 146–159.

Albrecht, G.L. and Devlieger, P.J. (1999) The disability paradox: high quality of life against all odds. *Social Science & Medicine*, 48(8), 977–978.

Ball, S.J. (2012) *Global Education Inc.: New Policy Networks and the Neo-liberal Imaginary*. London: Routledge.

——(2013) Education, justice and democracy: the struggle over ignorance and opportunity. Policy Paper, London, Centre for Labour and Social Studies. Available at: http://antiacademies.org.uk/wp-content/uploads/2013/10/ball-text.pdf (last accessed 25 March 2014).

Barnes, C. (2012) Understanding the social model of disability: past, present and future, in N. Watson, A. Roulstone and C. Thomas (eds) *The Routledge Handbook of Disability Studies*. London: Routledge, pp. 12–29.

Beckett, A.E. (2013) Nondisabled children's ideas about disability and disabled people. *British Journal of Sociology of Education*, DOI: 10.1080/01425692.2013.800444.

Beckett, A.E. and Buckner, L. (2012) Promoting positive attitudes towards disabled people: definition of, rationale and prospects for *anti-disablist* education. *British Journal of Sociology of Education*, 33(6), 873–891.

Beresford, B. (2012) Working on well-being: researchers' experiences of a participative approach to understanding the subjective well-being of disabled young people. *Children and Society*, 26, 234–240.

Beresford, B. and Rhodes, D. (2008) *Housing and Disabled Children*. York: Joseph Rowntree Foundation.

Bickenback, J.E., Chatterji, S., Badley E.M. and Ustun T.B. (1999) Models of disablement, universalism and the international classification of impairments, disabilities and handicaps. *Social Science and Medicine*, 48, 1173–1187.

Blackburn, C., Spencer, N. and Read, J. (2010) Prevalence of childhood disability and the characteristics and circumstances of disabled children in the UK: secondary analysis of the Family Resources Survey. *BMC Pediatrics*, 10, Article 21.

Blake, J.J., Lund, E.M., Zhou, Q., Kwok, O.M. and Benz, M.R. (2012) National prevalence rates of bully victimization among students with disabilities in the United States. *School Psychology Quarterly*, 27(4), 210–222.

Blatchford, P., Bassett, P., Brown, P., Koutsoubou, M., Martin, C., Russell, A. and Webster, R. with Rubie-Davies, C. (2009) The impact of support staff in schools. Results from the Deployment and Impact of Support Staff (DISS) project. (Strand 2 Wave 2), Research Report DCSF-RR148. London: DCSF.

Bragg, S. (2007) *Consulting Young People: A Review Of The Literature*. London: Creative Partnerships.

Brawn, E. and Rogers, C. (2012) *Keep Us Close: Ensuring Good, Inclusive and Accessible Local Services for Disabled Children and their Families*. London: Scope. Available at: www.scope. org.uk/sites/default/files/scope_keep_us_close_policy_report_final.pdf (last accessed 25 March 2014).

Briant, E., Watson, N. and Philo, G. (2011) Bad news for disabled people: how the newspapers are reporting disability. Project report. Strathclyde Centre for Disability Research and Glasgow Media Unit, University of Glasgow.

Bryson, C., Elam, G., Gray, M., Pickering, K., Purdon, S., Speight, S., Turley, C., Read, J., Blackburn, C., Spencer, N., Abbot, D. and Gordon, D. (2008) Development of a survey on services for disabled children. DCSF Research Report DCSF-RR053. Available at: www.gov.uk/government/uploads/system/uploads/attachment_data/file/ 222281/DCSF-RR053.pdf (last accessed 18 December 2013).

Bukowski, G., Roberts, H., Fraser, J. and Johnson, F. (2011) *The Equality Duties and Schools*. Equality and Human Rights Commission Research Report 70. Available at: www. equalityhumanrights.com/uploaded_files/research/rr70_equality_duties_and_schools. pdf (last accessed 1 June 2012).

Burchardt, T. (2005) *The Education and Employment of Disabled Young People: Frustrated Ambition*. Bristol: Policy Press.

Byrne, B. (2013) Hidden contradictions and conditionality: conceptualisations of inclusive education in international human rights law. *Disability & Society*, 28(2), 232–244.

Cabinet Office Prime Minister's Strategy Unit (2005) Improving the life chances of disabled people: final report. Available at: http://webarchive.nationalarchives.gov.uk/+/ http://www.cabinetoffice.gov.uk/media/cabinetoffice/strategy/assets/disability.pdf (last accessed 25 March 2014).

Cameron, L. and Murphy, J. (2002) Enabling young people with a learning disability to make choices at a time of transition. *British Journal of Learning Disabilities*, 30, 105–111.

Christensen, P. and James, A. (eds) (2008) *Research With Children, 2nd Edition: Perspectives and Practices*. London: Routledge.

Closs, A. (2000) *The Education of Children with Medical Conditions*. London: Fulton.

Cohen-Rottenberg, R. (2012) *Caught Inside a Paradox: How Cultural Representations Perpetuate Disability Stigma*. Available at: www.disabilityandrepresentation.com/caught-inside -a-paradox-how-cultural-representations-perpetuate-disability-stigma/ (last accessed 25 March 2014).

Connors, C. and Stalker, K. (2002) *Children's Experiences of Disability: A Positive Outlook*. Interchange 75. Edinburgh: Scottish Executive.

Cooke, P. and Standen, P.J. (2002) Abuse and disabled children: hidden needs...? *Child Abuse Review*, 11, 1–18.

Coster, W. and Khetani, M.A. (2008) Measuring participation of children with disabilities: issues and challenges. *Disability and Rehabilitation*, 30(8), 639–648.

Davis, J. and Watson, N. (2002) Countering stereotypes of disability: disabled children and resistance, in M. Corker and T. Shakespeare (eds) *Embodying Disability Theory*. London: Continuum, pp. 159–174.

Dearden, L., Miranda, A. and Rabehesketh, S. (2011) Measuring school value added with administrative data: the problem of missing variables. *Fiscal Studies*, 32(2), 263–278.

Department for Children, Schools and Families (DCSF) (2007) *Schools and Pupils in England*. January 2007 (Final) National Statistics First Release. Available at: www.dcsf.gov.uk/rsgateway/DB/SFR/s000744/UPDATEDSFR30_2007.pdf (last accessed 25 March 2014).

——(2008) Youth cohort study and longitudinal study of young people in England: the activities and experiences of 16 year olds: England 2007. Statistical Bulletin.

Department for Education (DfE) (2010) *Equality Act 2010: Advice For School Leaders, School Staff, Governing Bodies and Local Authorities*. Available at: www.education-advisors.com/wp-content/uploads/2012/03/Equality-Act-2010-advice-for-school-leaders-school-staff-governing-bodies-and-local-authorities.pdf (last accessed 1 June 2012).

——(2011a) *Support and Aspiration: A New Approach to Special Educational Needs and Disability*. London: DfE.

——(2011b) *Effectiveness of Child and Adolescent Mental Health Services (CAMHS)*. Statistics Release. London: DfE.

——(2012) *The Department and the Equality Act 2010: Equality Objectives 2012*. Available at: www.education.gov.uk/aboutdfe/policiesandprocedures/equalityanddiversity/b00202789/equality-commitments (last accessed 25 March 2014).

——(2013) *EQUALITY ACT 2010; Advice For School Leaders, School Staff, Governing Bodies and Local Authorities*. Available at: http://media.education.gov.uk/assets/files/pdf/e/equality%20act%20guidance%20february%202013.pdf (last accessed 25 March 2014).

Department for Education and Skills (DfES) (2001) *Special Educational Needs Code of Practice*. Nottingham: DfES.

——(2007) *Aiming High for Disabled Children: Better Support for Families*. London: DfES.

Department for Education and Skills and Disability Rights Commission (2006) *Implementing the Disability Discrimination Act in Schools and Early Years Settings*. Nottingham: DfES.

Department of Transport (2012) RAS30028 reported casulties by age, road user type and severity, Great Britain 2011. Available at: www.gov.uk/government/statistical-data-sets/road-accidents-and-safety-statistical-tables-index (last accessed 25 March 2014).

Department for Work and Pensions (DWP) (2012a) *Disability Facts and Figures*. Available at: http://odi.dwp.gov.uk/disability-statistics-and-research/disability-facts-and-figures.php (last accessed 25 March 2014).

——(2012b) *Fulfilling Potential Next Steps: DWP 2012*. Available at: http://odi.dwp.gov.uk/docs/fulfilling-potential/next-steps-rich-text.rtf (last accessed 25 March 2014).

——(2013) *Fulfilling Potential: Building a Deeper Understanding of Disability in the UK Today*. London: DWP. Available at: http://odi.dwp.gov.uk/docs/fulfilling-potential/building-understanding-main-report.pdf (last accessed 25 March 2014).

Dickinson, H., Parkinson, K., Ulrike Ravens-Sieberer, U., Schirripa, G., Thyen, U., Arnaud, C., Beckung, E., Fauconnier, J., McManus, V., Michelsen, S., Parkes, J. and

Colver, A.F. (2007) Self-reported quality of life of 8–12-year-old children with cerebral palsy: a cross-sectional European study. *The Lancet*, 369(9580), 2171–2178.

Disability Rights Commission (DRC) (2002) *Disability Discrimination Act 1995 Part 4: Code of Practice for Schools*. Available at: www.equalityhumanrights.com/uploaded_files/drc_schools_code.pdf (last accessed 25 March 2014).

——(2005) *Disability in Scotland 2005–2020: A State of the Nation Report. Making Rights a Reality*. Edinburgh: Scottish Council Foundation.

Emerson, E. (2012) Understanding disabled childhoods: what can we learn from population-based studies? *Children & Society*, 26, 214–222.

Evangelou, M., Taggart, B., Sylva, K., Melhuish, E., Sammons, P. and Siraj-Blatchford, I. (2008) *What Makes a Successful Transition from Primary to Secondary School?* Research Report DCSF-RR019. London: DCSF.

Farrell, P., Alborz, A., Howes, A. and Pearson, D. (2010) The impact of teaching assistants on improving pupils' academic achievement in mainstream schools: a review of the literature. *Educational Review*, 62(4), 435–448.

Fielding, M. and Moss, P.P. (2011) *Radical Education and the Common School*. London: Routledge.

Finkelstein, V. (2001) *The Social Model of Disability Repossessed*. Available at: http://disability-studies.leeds.ac.uk/files/library/finkelstein-soc-mod-repossessed.pdf (last accessed 25 March 2014).

——(2004) Prepresenting disability, in J. Swain (ed.) *Disabling Barriers, Enabling Environments*. 2nd Edition. London: Sage, pp. 13–20.

——(2007) *The 'Social Model of Disability' and the Disability Movement*. Available at: http://disability-studies.leeds.ac.uk/files/library/finkelstein-The-Social-Model-of-Disability-and-the-Disability-Movement.pdf (last accessed 25 March 2014).

Fitzgerald, H. (2012) Paralympic athletes and 'knowing disability'. *International Journal of Disability, Development and Education*, 59(3), 243–255.

Florian, L., Devecchi, C. and Dee, L. (2008) How can the capability approach contribute to understanding provision for people with learning difficulties? *Prospero*, 14(1), 24–33.

Flutter, J. and Ruddock, J. (2004) *Consulting Pupils: What's in it for Schools?* London: RoutledgeFalmer.

Fraser, C. and Meadows, S. (2008) Children's views of Teaching Assistants in primary schools. *Education 3–13: International Journal of Primary, Elementary and Early Years Education*, 36(4), 351–363.

French, S. (1993) Disability, impairment or something in between?, in J. Swain, V. Finkelstein, S. French and M. Oliver (eds) *Disabling Barriers—Enabling Environments*. Thousand Oaks, CA: Sage Publications, pp. 17–25.

Garthwaite, K. (2011) 'The language of shirkers and scroungers?' Talking about illness, disability and coalition welfare reform. *Disability & Society*, 26, 369–372.

Georgeson, J. (2012) Methodological issues in accessing children's views: using interviews and questionnaires. *Procedia – Social and Behavioral Sciences*, 47, 1605–1609.

Gleeson, B. (1999) *Geographies of Disability*. London: Routledge.

Goodley, D. and Roets, G. (2008) The becomings and goings of 'developmental disabilities': the cultural politics of 'impairment' discourse. *Studies in the Cultural Politics of Education*, 29(2), 239–255.

Gorard, S. (2010) Serious doubts about school effectiveness. *British Educational Research Journal*, 36(5), 745–766.

——(2011) Now you see it, now you don't: school effectiveness as conjuring? *Research in Education*, 86, 39–45.

——(2012) Who is eligible for free school meals? Characterising free school meals as a measure of disadvantage in England. *British Educational Research Journal*, 38(6), 1003–1017.

Government Equality Office (2010) *Equality Act 2010*. Available at: www.equalities.gov. uk/equality_act_2010.aspx (last accessed 25 March 2014).

Grant, C. and Hamlyn, B. (2008/9) *Services for Disabled Children*. Draft report for DCSF.

——(2009) *Parental Experience of Services for Disabled Children: National Survey*. Nottingham: DCSF Publications.

Great Britain (1995) *Disability Discrimination Act 1995*. London: HMSO.

——(2005) *Disability Discrimination Act 2005*. London: The Stationery Office.

——(2012) *Draft Legislation on Reform of Provision for Children and Young People with Special Educational Needs*. London: The Stationery Office.

Green, H., McGinnity, A., Meltzer, H., Ford, T. and Goodman, R. (2005) *Mental Health of Children and Young People in Great Britain, 2004*. Summary report. A survey carried out by the Office for National Statistics on behalf of the Department of Health and Scottish Executive. London: HMSO.

Green, R., Collingwood, A. and Ross, A. (2010) Characteristics of bullying victims in schools. Research Report DFE-RR001. DfE. Available at: www.gov.uk/government/uploads/system/uploads/attachment_data/file/182409/DFE-RR001.pdf (last accessed 24 March 2014).

Gronvig, L. (2008) Definitions of disability in social sciences: methodological perspectives. *Scandinavian Journal of Disability Research*, 10(2), 144–146.

Gustavvson, A., Tossebro, J. and Traustadottir, R. (2005) Introduction: approaches and perspectives in Nordic disability research, in A. Gustavvson, J. Sandvin, R. Traustadottir and J. Tossebro (eds) *Resistance, Reflection and Change: Nordic Disability Research*. Sweden: Studentlitteratur, pp. 23–44.

Hackett, L., Theodosiou, L., Bond, C., Blackburn, C., Spicer, F. and Lever, R. (2010) Mental health needs in schools for emotional, behavioural and social difficulties. *British Journal of Special Education*, 37(3), 154–155.

Hallam, S. (2009) An evaluation of the Social and Emotional Aspects of Learning (SEAL) programme: promoting positive behaviour, effective learning and well-being in primary school children. *Oxford Review of Education*, 35(3), 313–330.

Hill, M. (2006) Children's voices on ways of having a voice: children's and young people's perspectives on methods used in research and consultation. *Childhood*, 13, 69–89.

Ho, A. (2004) To be labelled, or not to be labelled: that is the question. *British Journal of Learning Disabilities*, 32, 86–92.

Holt, L. (2010) Young people's embodied social capital and performing disability. *Children's Geographies*, 8(1), 25–37.

Howes, A., Farrell, P., Kaplan, I. and Moss, S. (2003) *The Impact of Paid Adult Support on the Participation and Learning of Pupils in Mainstream Schools*. London: Institute of Education, Evidence for Policy and Practice Information and Co-ordinating Centre.

Hughes, L.A., Banks, P. and Terras, M.M. (2013) Secondary school transition for children with special educational needs: a literature review. *Support for Learning*, 28(1), 24–34.

Humphrey, N. and Squires, G. (2011). *Achievement for All National Evaluation: Final Report*. DfE RR 176 Department for Education. Available at: www.gov.uk/government/

uploads/system/uploads/attachment_data/file/193254/DFE-RR176.pdf (last accessed 25 March 2014).

Humphrey, N., Lendrum, A. and Wigelsworth, M. (2010) Social and emotional aspects of learning (SEAL) programme in secondary schools: national evaluation. Research Report DFE-RR049.

Hutchison T. and Gordon, D. (2005) Ascertaining the prevalence of childhood disability. *Child: Care, Health and Development*, 31(1), 99–107.

IPPR (2007) *DISABILITY 2020: Opportunities for the Full and Equal Citizenship of Disabled People in Britain in 2020*. Available at: www.ippr.org.uk/members/download.asp?f=/ecomm/files/Disability_2020_full.pdf&a=login#login (last accessed 1 October 2010).

Irwin, M. (2013) 'Hanging out with mates': friendship quality and its effect on academic endeavours and social behaviours. *Australian Journal of Education*, 57, 141.

Kelly, A. and Downey, C. (2010) Value-added measures for schools in England: looking inside the 'black box' of complex metrics. *Educational Assessment, Evaluation and Accountability*, 22, 181–198.

King, M. and King, D. (2006) How the law defines the special educational needs of autistic children. *Child and Family Law Quarterly*, 18(1), 23–42.

Kounali, D., Robinson, A., Goldstein, H. and Lauder, H. (submitted for publication) The probity of free school meals as a proxy measure for disadvantage, University of Bath, Maths/Education. Available at: www.bristol.ac.uk/cmm/publications/fsm.pdf (last accessed 25 March 2014).

Laevers, F., Vandebussche, E., Kog, M. and Depondt, L. (2002) A process-oriented child monitoring system for young children. Centre for Experiential Education.

Lamb, B. (2009) *Lamb Inquiry. Special Educational Needs and Parental Confidence*. Report to the Secretary of State on the Lamb Inquiry Review of SEN and Disability Information. Available at: http://webarchive.nationalarchives.gov.uk/20100202100434/http://dcsf.gov.uk/lambinquiry/downloads/Lamb%20Inquiry%20Review%20of%20SEN%20and%20Disability%20Information.pdf (last accessed 3 September 2012).

——(2011) Support and aspiration: cultural revolution or pragmatic evolution? Chapter 2: Policy Paper 6, SEN Green Paper: progress and prospects 6th Series, June 2011. SEN Policy Options Group.

Langlois, R. (2002) Global measures of disability statistics: Canada's experiences so far… Paper presented to the First Meeting of the Washington Group on Disability Measurement, 18–20 February 2002.

Larkins, C., Thomas, N., Judd, D., Lloyd, J., Carter, B., Farrelly, N., Carr, Z., Carr, D, Finch, W.J., Onia, A., Reed, E., Sheehan, D., Titterington, R., Winstanley, R. with Carroll, L., Burgess, N. and Mundry, H. (2013) 'We want to help people see things our way'. A rights-based analysis of disabled children's experience living with low income. London: Office of the Children's Commissioner.

Lauder, H., Kounali, D., Robinson, T. and Goldstein, H. (2010) Pupil composition and accountability: an analysis in English primary schools. *International Journal of Educational Research*, 49, 49–68.

Lewis, A. (2004) 'And when did you last see your father?' Exploring the views of children with learning difficulties/disabilities. *British Journal of Special Education*, 3(1), 4–10.

——(2011) Disabled children's 'voice' and experiences, in S. Haines and D. Ruebain (eds) *Education, Disability and Social Policy*. Bristol: Policy Press, pp. 89–104.

Lewis, A., Robertson, C. and Parsons, S. (2005) Experiences of disabled students and their families. Phase 1. Research report to Disability Rights Commission, June 2005.

Birmingham: University of Birmingham, School of Education. Available at: http://83.137.212.42/sitearchive/DRC/library/research/education/experiences_of_disabled.html (last accessed 25 March 2014).

Lewis, A.L., Davison, I.W., Ellins, J.M., Parsons, S. and Robertson, C.M.L. (2006) Survey of parents and carers of disabled children and young people in Great Britain. Research report to Disability Rights Commission, The University of Birmingham, School of Education.

Lewis, A., Davison, I., Ellins, J., Parsons, S., Robertson, C. and Sharpe, J. (2007) The experiences of disabled pupils and their families. *British Journal of Special Education*, 34, 189–195.

Lowson, K. and Mahon, J. (2009) *Aiming High for Disabled Children: Improving Data. Final Report.* London: DoH. Available at: http://php.york.ac.uk/inst/yhec/files/resources/FinalReport-Nov09.pdf (last accessed 25 March 2014).

MacArthur, J. (2013) Sustaining friendships, relationships, and rights at school. *International Journal of Inclusive Education*, 17(8), 793–811.

McKenna, K. and Day, L. (2010) *Parents' and Young People's Complaints about Schools Research.* Report DFE-RR193. London: DFE.

McLaughlin, C. and Clarke, B. (2010) Relational matters: a review of the impact of school experience on mental health in early adolescence. *Educational and Child Psychology*, 27(1), 95–107.

Maras, P. and Aveling, E. (2006) Students with special educational needs: transitions from primary to secondary school. *British Journal of Special Education*, 33(4), 196–203.

Martin, N.T., Bibby, P., Mudford, O.C. and Eikeseth, S. (2003) Toward the use of a standardized assessment for young people with autism: current assessment practices in the UK. *Autism*, 7(3), 321–330.

Mitra, S. (2006) The capability approach and disability. *Journal of Disability Policy Studies*, 16(4), 236–247.

Mont, D. (2007) Measuring disability prevalence. Social Protection Discussion Paper No. 0706. Washington, DC: The World Bank, OECD.

Mooney, A., Owen, C. and Statham, J. (2008) *Disabled Children: Numbers, Characteristics and Local Service Provision.* Research report DCSF-RP042. Nottingham: DCFS.

Moore, M. and Slee, R. (2012) Disability studies, inclusive education and exclusion, in N. Watson, A. Roulstone and C. Thomas (eds) *The Routledge Handbook of Disability Studies.* London: Routledge, pp. 225–239.

Naraian, S. (2011) Teacher discourse, peer relations, significant disability: unraveling one friendship story. *International Journal of Qualitative Studies in Education*, 24(1), 97–115.

Naylor, P., Dawson, J., Emerson, E. and Tantam, D. (2012) *Prevalence of Bullying in Secondary School by SEN Type: Analysis of Combined NPD and LSYPE Data Files.* End of Award Report to ESRC. Swindon: ESRC.

Norwich, B. (2008) *Dilemmas of Difference, Inclusion and Disability: International Perspectives and Future Directions.* London: Routledge.

——(2012) An overview of issues emerging as the policy context changes, in SEN Policy Research Forum, The Coalition Government's policy on SEND: aspirations and challenges? JORSEN doi: 10.1111/1471-3802.12027.

Nuffield Foundation (2012) *Social Trends and Mental Health: Introducing the Main Findings.* London: Nuffield Foundation.

OECD (2004) *Equity in Education: Students with Disabilities, Learning Difficulties and Disadvantages.* Paris: OECD.

Office of Children's Commissioner (OCC) (2011) *The Story so Far*. UK Children's Commissioners' Midterm report to the UK State Party on the UN Convention on the Rights of the Child. London: OCC.

Office for Disability Issues (2007) Future challenges: *should* we count them, an UDI perspective. Presentation by Grahame Whitfield at Warwick University on 14 March 2014 at the conference, Can We Count Them: Disabled Children and Their Households?

——(2010) *Equality Act 2010 Guidance: Guidance on Matters to be Taken into Account in Determining Questions Relating to the Definition of Disability*. Available at: http://odi.dwp.gov.uk/docs/wor/new/ea-guide.pdf (last accessed 25 March 2014).

——(2011) *On the UN Convention on the Rights of Persons with Disabilities*. Available at: http://odi.dwp.gov.uk/docs/disabled-people-and-legislation/uk-initial-report.pdf (last accessed 25 March 2014).

Office for National Statistics (ONS) (2004) *The Health of Children and Young People*. Available at: www.statistics.gov.uk/children/downloads/disability.pdf (last accessed 1 October 2010).

——(2005) *General Household Survey, 2005 Report, Appendix E*. Available at: www.ons.gov.uk/ons/rel/ghs/general-household-survey/2005-report/index.html (last accessed 8 July 2014).

——(2011a) *Harmonised Concepts and Questions for Social Data Sources: Primary Standards Version 1.0*.

——(2011b) *Life Opportunities Survey: Analysis of Barriers to Participation across a Range of Life Areas 2009/10*.

——(2012) *Opinions Survey: July, August, September 2012, Appendix. Table 48.1–48.4*.

——(undated) *Family Resources Survey Question Instructions: Household Schedule Benefit Unit Schedule 2004–2005 Version*. Available at: www.esds.ac.uk/doc/5291/mrdoc/pdf/5291 userguide3.pdf (last accessed 8 July 2014).

Ofsted (2010) *SEN and Disability Review: A Statement Is Not Enough*. London: Ofsted.

——(2011) *Schools and Parents*. Manchester: Ofsted.

——(2012) *Protecting Disabled Children: Thematic Inspection*. Available at: www.ofsted.gov.uk/resources/protecting-disabled-children-thematic-inspection (last accessed 25 March 2014).

——(2013) *School Inspection Handbook*. Available at: www.ofsted.gov.uk/resources/school-inspection-handbook (last accessed 25 March 2014).

Oliver, M. (1983) *Social Work with Disabled People*. Basingstoke: Macmillan.

——(1990) The individual and social models of disability. Paper presented at Joint Workshop of the Living Options Group and the Research Unit of the Royal College of Physicians on People With Established Locomotor Disabilities In Hospitals, 23 July 1990. Available at: http://disability-studies.leeds.ac.uk/files/library/Oliver-in-soc-dis.pdf (last accessed 25 March 2014).

——(1996) *Understanding Disability*. Basingstoke: Macmillan.

——(2004) The social model in action: if I had a hammer, in C. Barnes and G. Mercer (eds) *Implementing the Social Model of Disability: Theory and Research*. Leeds: The Disability Press, pp. 18–31.

Opinion Leader (2009) *Time to Talk Parents as Partners: Deliberative Event Research Report*. Nottingham: DCSF Publications

ORB (2004) Who do they think they are? Unpublished. London: Disability Rights Commission. Cited by DRC (2005) *Disability in Scotland 2005–2020: A State of the Nation Report*. Available at: http://disability-studies.leeds.ac.uk/files/library/DRC-DRC-Scotland-2005-2020.pdf (last accessed 25 March 2014).

Parsons, S., Lewis, A., Davison, I., Ellins, J. and Robertson, C. (2009a) Satisfaction with educational provision for children with SEN or disabilities: a national postal survey of the views of parents in Great Britain. *Educational Review*, 61(1), 19–47.

Parsons, S., Lewis, A. and Ellins, J. (2009b) The views and experiences of parents of children with autistic spectrum disorder about educational provision: comparison with parents of children with other disabilities from an online survey. *European Journal of Special Needs Education*, 24(1), 37–58.

Pedder, D. and McIntyre, D. (2006) Pupil consultation: the importance of social capital. *Education Review*, 58, 145–157.

Pellegrini, A.D. (2002) Bullying, victimization, and sexual harassment during the transition to middle school. *Educational Psychologist*, 37(3), 151–163.

Peuravaara, K. (2013) Theorizing the body: conceptions of disability,gender and normality. *Disability & Society*, 28(3), 408–417.

Pivik, J., Mccomas, J. and Laflamme, M. (2002) Barriers and facilitators to inclusive education. *Exceptional Children*, 69(1), 97–107.

Porter, J. (2011) The challenge of using multiple methods to gather the views of children, in H. Daniels and M. Hedegaard Vygotsky (eds) *Special Needs Education: Rethinking Support for Children and Schools*. London: Continuum, pp. 30–47.

——(2013) Be careful how you ask! Using focus groups and nominal group technique to explore the barriers to learning. *International Journal on Research Methods in Education*, 36(1), 33–51.

——(2014) Research and pupil voice, in L. Florian (ed.) *Handbook of Special Education*, 2nd Edition. London: Sage, pp. 405–420.

Porter, J., Daniels, H., Feiler, A. and Georgeson, J. (2011) Collecting disability data from parents. *Research Papers in Education*, 26(4), 427–443.

Porter, J., Daniels, H., Martin, S., Hacker, J., Feiler, A. and Georgeson, G. (2010) *Testing of Disability Identification Tool for Schools*. Research Report DFE-RR025. Available at: www.education.gov.uk/publications/RSG/AllPublications/Page1/DFE-RR025 (last accessed 25 March 2014).

Porter, J., Daniels, H., Georgeson, J., Feiler, A., Hacker, J., with Tarleton, B., Gallop, V. and Watson, D. (2008) *Disability Data Collection for Children's Services*. Nottingham: DCFS.

Powell, R., Smith, R., Jones, G. and Reakes, A. (2006) *Transition from Primary to Secondary School: Current Arrangements and Good Practice in Wales*. Slough, Berks: National Foundation for Educational Research.

Preece, D. and Jordan, R. (2010) Obtaining the views of children and young people with autism spectrum disorders about their experience of daily life and social care support. *British Journal of Learning Disabilities*, 38, 10–20.

Pullin, D.C. (2008) Implications for human and civil rights entitlements: stigma, steroetypes, and civil rights in disability classification systems, in L. Florian and M.J. McLaughlin (eds) *Disability Classification in Education: Issues and Perspectives*. California: Corwin Press, pp. 78–93.

Read, J., Blackburn, C. and Spencer, N. (2009) Disabled children in the UK: a quality assessment of quantitative data sources. *Child: Care, Health and Development*, 36(1), 130–141.

Read, J., Spencer, N. and Blackburn, C. (2007) *Can We Count Them? Disabled Children and Their Households*. Full Project Report to the ESRC Award No. Res-000-22-1725. Swindon: ESRC.

Rees, S.A. (2007) Understanding instruction: how severely brain injured pupils make meaning in the mainstream secondary classroom. PhD. University of Bath.

Reeve, D. (2012) Psycho-emotional disablism: the missing link?, in N. Watson, A. Roulstone and C. Thomas (eds) *The Routledge Handbook of Disability Studies*. London: Routledge, pp. 78–92.

Reindal, S.M. (2008) A social relational model of disability: a theoretical framework for special needs education? *European Journal of Special Needs Education*, 23(2), 135–146.

——(2010a) What is the purpose? Reflections on inclusion and special education from a capability perspective. *European Journal of Special Needs Education*, 25(1), 1–12.

——(2010b) Redefining disability: a rejoinder to a critique. *Nordic Journal of Applied Ethics / ETIKKIPRAKSIS*, 1, 125–135.

Rhodes, P., Nocon, A., Small, N. and Wright, J. (2008) Disability and identity: the challenge of epilepsy. *Disability & Society*, 23(4), 385–395.

Riddell, S. and Watson, N. (2003) Disability, culture and identity: an introduction, in S. Riddell and N. Watson (eds) *Disability Culture and Identity*. Harlow: Pearson, pp. 1–18.

Riddell, S., Harris, N., Smith, E. and Weedon, E. (2010) Dispute resolution in additional and special educational needs: local authority perspectives. *Journal of Education Policy*, 25(1), 55–71.

Rieser, R. (1990) Internalized oppression: how it seems to me, in R. Rieser and M. Mason (eds) *Disability Equality in Education*. London: ILEA, pp. 29–32.

Robinson, V. (2009) Why do some policies not work in schools, in H. Daniels, H. Lauder and J. Porter (eds) *Knowledge, Values and Educational Policy: A Critical Perspective*. London: Routledge, pp. 237–252.

Robson, C. and Evans, P. (2003) *Educating Children with Disabilities in Developing Countries: The Role of Data Sets*. Huddersfield: OECD.

Rose, C. (2006) *Do You Have a Disability – Yes or No? Or Is There a Better Way of Asking? Guidance on Disability Disclosure and Respecting Confidentiality*. London: Learning and Skills Council.

Rouse, M., Henderson, K. and Danielson, L. (2008) Concluding thoughts: on perspectives and purposes of disability classification systems in education, in L. Florian and M. McLaughlin (eds) *Disability Classification in Education: Issues and Perspectives*. Thousand Oaks, CA: Corwin Press, pp. 263–268.

Runswick-Cole, K. (2007) 'The Tribunal was the most stressful thing: more stressful than my son's diagnosis or behaviour': the experiences of families who go to the Special Educational Needs and Disability Tribunal (SENDisT). *Disability & Society*, 22(3), 315–328.

Rutherford, G. (2011) Doing right by teacher aides, students with disabilities, and relational social justice. *Harvard Educational Review*, 81, 95–118.

Shakespeare, T. (1994) Cultural representation of disabled people: dustbins for disavowal? *Disability & Society*, 9(3), 283–299.

——(1996) Disability, identity and difference, in C. Barnes and G. Mercer (eds) *Exploring the Divide*. Leeds: The Disability Press, pp. 94–113.

——(2006) *Disability Rights and Wrongs*. London: Routledge.

——(2008) Debating disability. *Journal of Medical Ethics*, 34, 11–14.

——(2012) Disability in developing countries, in N. Watson, A. Roulstone and C. Thomas (eds) *The Routledge Handbook of Disability Studies*. London: Routledge, pp. 12–29.

Shakespeare, T. and Watson, N. (2002) The social model of disability: an outdated ideology? *Research in Social Science and Disability*, 2, 9–28.

Sheldon, A., Traustadóttir, R., Beresford, P., Boxall, K. and Oliver, M. (2007) Disability rights and wrongs? *Disability & Society*, 22(2), 209–234.

Skånfors, L. (2009) Ethics in child research: children's agency and researchers' 'ethical radar', *Childhoods Today*, 3(1), 1–22.

Skar, R.N.L. (2003) Peer and adult relationships of adolescents with disabilities. *Journal of Adolescence*, 26, 635–649.

Skryabina, E. (2014) School Pedagogic Practices and Effectiveness of the Universal School-based CBT Program FRIENDS. Presentation at the University of Oxford, School of Education, January 2014.

Slade, Z., Coulter, A. and Joyce, L. (2009) *Parental Experience of Services for Disabled Children – Qualitative Research*. DCSF-RR147. London: DCSF.

Smith, B. and Sparkes, A.C. (2012) Disability, sport and physical activity: a critical review, in N. Watson, A. Roulstone and C. Thomas (eds) *The Routledge Handbook of Disability Studies*. London: Routledge, pp. 336–347.

Spencer, N., Devereux, E., Wallace, A., Sundrum, R., Shenoy, M., Bacchus, C. and Logan, S. (2005) Disabling conditions and registration for child abuse and neglect: a population based study. *Paediatrics*, 116, 609–613.

Stallard, P., Skryabina, E., Taylor, G., Phillips, R., Daniels, H., Anderson, R. and Simpson, N. (submitted for publication). Anxiety prevention in schools: a cluster randomised controlled trial of a universally delivered cognitive behaviour therapy programme (FRIENDS).

Stobbs, P. (2012) Overview of previous national SEND achievements and their fit with current SEN policy directions, in The Coalition Government's policy on SEND: aspirations and challenges? SEN Policy Research Forum. JORSEN doi: 10.1111/1471-3802.12027.

Symes, W. and Humphrey, N. (2012) Including pupils with autistic spectrum disorders in the classroom: the role of teaching assistants. *European Journal of Special Needs Education*, 27(4), 517–532.

Terzi, L. (2005) A capability perspective on impairment, disability and special needs: towards social justice in education. *Theory and Research in Education*, 3, 197.

——(2007) Capability and educational equality: the just distribution of resources to students with disabilities and special educational needs. *Journal of Philosophy of Education*, 41(4), 757–773.

——(2008) Beyond the dilemmas of difference: the capability approach in disability and special educational needs, in L. Florian and M.J. McLaughlin (eds) *Disability Classification in Education: Issues and Perspectives*. Thousand Oaks, CA: Corwin, pp. 244–262.

Thomas, C. (2004) Developing the social relational in the social model of disability: a theoretical agenda, in C. Barnes and G. Mercer (eds) *Implementing the Social Model of Disability: Theory and Research*. Leeds: The Disability Press, pp. 32–47.

Thomas, N. and O'Kane, C. (1998) *Children and Decision Making: A Summary Report*. University of Wales Swansea: International Centre for Childhood Studies.

Tribunals Statistics Quarterly (2013) 1 July to 30 September 2012, published January 2013 by Ministry of Justice. Available at: www.justice.gov.uk/downloads/statistics/tribs-stats/quarterly-tribs-q2-2012-13.pdf (last accessed 25 March 2014).

Tufvesson, C. and Tufvesson, J. (2009) The building process as a tool towards an all-inclusive school: a Swedish example focusing on children with defined concentration difficulties such as ADHD, autism and Down's syndrome. *Journal of Housing and the Built Environment*, 24, 47–66.

Ullenhag, A., Bult, M.K., Nyquist, A., Ketelaar, M., Jansen, R., Krumlinde-Sundholm, L., Almquist, L. and Grandlund, M. (2012) An international comparison of patterns of participation in leisure activities for children with and without disabilities in Sweden, Norway and the Netherlands. *Developmental Neurohabilitation*, 15(5), 369–385.

Unicef (2012) *Two Stage Child Disability Study: Bhutan 2010–2011*. Bhutan: National Statistics Bureau.

United Nations (2006) *United Nations Convention on the Rights of Persons with Disabilities.* Available at: www.un.org/disabilities/convention/conventionfull.shtml (last accessed 25 March 2014).

——(2011) *Disability and the Millennium Development Goals: A Review of the MDG Process and Strategies for Inclusion of Disability Issues in Millennium Development Goal Efforts.* New York: United Nations. Available at: www.un.org/disabilities/documents/review_of_disability_and_the_mdgs.pdf (last accessed 25 March 2014).

Waddell, G. and Aylward, M. (2010) *Models of Sickness and Disability Applied to Common Health Problems.* London: Royal Society of Medicine Press Ltd.

Watson, N. (1999) *Life as a Disabled Child: A Qualitative Study of Young People's Experiences and Perspectives.* Final report for the ESRC. Available at: www.esrcsocietytoday.ac.uk/ESRCInfoCentre/ViewAwardPage.aspx?data=z8HSvl3fWwVY2sDo4JNP8iOLJQdQnq85gWScqW%2FOpI2%2B5YiUw2%2BKJTJyRuKMeMICf1M%2BXm3GT0nPA52slwsnHEgtdyAN3GYpZpdo8Nagi7c%3D&xu=0&isAwardHolder=&isProfiled=&AwardHolderID=&Sector (last accessed 1 September 2009).

——(2002) Well, I know this is going to sound very strange to you, but I don't see myself as a disabled person: identity and disability. *Disability & Society*, 17(5), 509–527.

——(2004) The dialectics of disability: a social model for the 21st Century?, in C. Barnes and G. Mercer (eds) *Implementing the Social Model of Disability: Theory and Research.* Leeds: The Disability Press, pp. 101–117.

——(2012) Theorising the lives of disabled children: how can disability theory help? *Children and Society*, 26(3), 192–202.

Webster, R. and Blatchford, P. (2013) The Making a Statement project: final report. A study of the teaching and support experienced by pupils with a statement of special educational needs in mainstream primary schools. London: IOE. Available at: www.nuffieldfoundation.org/sites/default/files/files/mastreport.pdf (last accessed 25 March 2014).

Webster, R., Blatchford, P., Bassett, P., Brown, P., Martin, C. and Russell, R. (2010) Double standards and first principles: framing teaching assistant support for pupils with special educational needs. *European Journal of Special Needs Education*, 25(4), 319–336.

Wedell, K.(2008) Evolving dilemmas about classification, in L. Florian and M. McLaughlin (eds) *Disability Classification in Education: Issues and Perspectives.* Thousand Oaks, CA: Corwin Press, pp. 47–67.

Weller, S. (2007) 'Sticking with your mates?' Children's friendship trajectories during the transition from primary to secondary school. *Children & Society*, 21, 339–351.

Welsh Assembly Government (2008) *We Are On the Way.* No longer available. Mentioned at: www.childreninwales.org.uk/news-archive/we-are-on-the-way-policy-agenda-in-wales-for-disabled-children-and-young-people-launched-031208-w (last accessed 7 July 2014).

——(2011) *The Journey so Far: An Update to the Policy Agenda 'We are on the Way' Aimed to Transform the Lives of Disabled Children and Young People.* Available at: http://wales.gov.uk/docs/dcells/publications/110412journeysofaren.pdf (last accessed 4 July 2014).

Westbrook, L.E., Silvere, E.J. and Stein, R.E. (1998) Implications for estimates of disability in children: a comparison of definitional components. *Pediatrics*, 101(6), 1025–1030.

Whitaker, P. (2007) Provision for youngsters with autistic spectrum disorders in mainstream schools: what parents say – and what parents want. *British Journal of Special Education*, 34(3), 170–178.

White-Koning, M., Arnaud, C., Bourdet-Loubère, S., Bazex, H., Colver, A. and Grandjean, H. (2005) Subjective quality of life in children with intellectual impairment: how can it be assessed? *Developmental Medicine and Child Neurology*, 47, 281–285.

Williams, A. (2012) Paralympics 2012: it cannot be something that is just every four years. *Guardian*, 9 September. Available at: www.guardian.co.uk/sport/blog/2012/sep/09/paralympics-2012-funding-athletes (last accessed 25 March 2014).

Wolf, F., Guevara, J.P., Grum, C.M., Clark, N.M. and Cates, C.J. (2008) Educational interventions for asthma in children. *Cochrane Database of Systematic Reviews 2002*, Issue 4. Art. No.: CD000326. DOI: 10.1002/14651858.CD000326. The Cochrane Collaboration. Published by John Wiley & Sons, Ltd. Available at: http://onlinelibrary.wiley.com/doi/10.1002/14651858.CD000326/pdf/standard (last accessed 3 May 2012).

World Health Organization (WHO) (1995) The World Health Organization Quality of Life assessment (WHOQOL): position paper from the World Health Organization. *Social Science & Medicine*, 41(10), 1403–1409.

——(2001) *International Classification of Functioning, Disability and Health. (ICF).* Geneva: WHO.

——(2007) *International Classification of Functioning, Disability and Health. (ICF-CY).* Geneva: WHO.

World Health Organization and World Bank (2011) *World Report on Disability.* Geneva: WHO.

Yantzi, N.M., Young, N.L. and Mckeever, P. (2010) The suitability of school playgrounds for physically disabled children. *Children's Geographies*, 8(1), 65–78.

Young, N.L., Williams, J.I., Yoshida, K.K., Bombardier, C. and Wright, J.G. (1996) The context of measuring disability: does it matter whether capability or performance is measured? *Journal of Clinical Epidemiology*, 49(10), 1097–1101.

Ytterhus, B. (2012) Everyday segregation amongst disabled children and their peers: a qualitative longitudinal study in Norway. *Children & Society*, 26, 203–213.

Index